THE MAD OFFICIALS

Also by Christopher Booker

*The Neophiliacs: a study of the revolution
in English life in the 50s and 60s*
Goodbye London (with Candida Lycett-Green)
The Booker Quiz
The Seventies
The Games War: a Moscow journal

THE MAD OFFICIALS

Christopher Booker
AND
Richard North

Illustrated by
Willie Rushton

Constable · London

First published in Great Britain 1994
by Constable and Company Limited
3 The Lanchesters, 162 Fulham Palace Road
London W6 9ER
Copyright © 1994 by Christopher Booker and Richard North
Illustrations copyright © 1994 by Willie Rushton
The right of Christopher Booker and Richard North to be
identified as the authors of this work
has been asserted by them in accordance
with the Copyright, Designs and Patents Act 1988
ISBN 0 09 473200 0
Set in Linotron Sabon 10½pt by
Rowland Phototypesetting Limited
Bury St Edmunds, Suffolk
Printed in Great Britain by
St Edmundsbury Press Limited
Bury St Edmunds, Suffolk

A CIP catalogue record for this book
is available from the British Library

'I should not be surprised if the law were like that: because in modern England there is practically no law to be surprised at'

The Mad Official
G. K. Chesterton

CONTENTS

GLOSSARY

CAP	Common Agricultural Policy
CFP	Common Fisheries Policy
DH	Department of Health
D.o.E	Department of the Environment
D.o.T.	Department of Transport
DTI	Department of Trade and Industry
EEC	European Economic Community
EHO	Environmental Health Officer
EPA	Environmental Protection Act
HMIP	Her Majesty's Inspectorate of Pollution
HSE	Health and Safety Executive
LACOTS	Local Authority Co-ordinating body on Trading Standards
MAFF	Ministry of Agriculture, Fisheries and Food
NRA	National Rivers Authority
OPs	Organo-Phosphorus compounds/chemicals
VMD	Veterinary Medicines Directorate
VPC	Veterinary Products Committee
VOCs	Volatile Organic Compounds
WRA	Waste Regulation Authority

Much of the regulatory onslaught of 1992/3 derived from a combination of two factors:
1. the enormous increase in directives and regulations from the EEC;
2. a succession of major new Acts of Parliament, mostly passed in the closing years of the Thatcher Government.

The Brussels directives in turn each had to be implemented in the form of new UK regulations, many of which were introduced under new or recent British statutes.

Among the more important of the measures creating the regulatory explosion of 1992/3 were:

Hygiene
Food Safety Act 1990.
This quickly spawned a mass of subsidiary regulations, including the Food Hygiene (Amendment) Regulations 1990 and 1991; the Fresh Meat (Hygiene and Inspection) Regulations 1992, implementing EEC Directive 91/497; and the Fisheries Products Regulations, implementing EEC Directive 91/493.

Safety
Health and Safety at Work Act 1974.
Although this had been on the statute book for nearly twenty years, it now gave rise to a mass of new regulations, including the Control of Substances Hazardous to Health Regulations (COSHH) 1988, implementing directive 80/1107; the Electricity at Work Regulations 1988; and in 1992 no fewer than

six new sets of health and safety at work regulations implementing EEC directives, on such matters as Manual Handling, Visual Display Screens, Personal Protective Equipment and Provision and Use of Work Equipment.

Environment

Environmental Protection Act 1990.

This also soon created a mass of subsidiary regulations such as the Waste Management Regulations 1991 and the Environmental Protection (Prescribed Processes and Substances) Regulations 1991, implementing a string of EEC directives such as 84/360 on industrial air pollution, 91/156 on waste disposal and 91/157 on the collection and recycling of batteries.

The Water Resources Act 1991 and other measures also created a mass of new regulations related to water quality, such as the Private Water Supplies Regulations 1991, implementing the many EEC water directives, such as 80/778 on drinking water.

Care

Children Act 1989.

Community Care Act 1990.

Although these had nothing to do with the EEC, they each created their own new thicket of regulatory law.

Consumer Protection

Financial Services Act 1986.

Consumer Protection Act 1987. This produced a mass of regulations including the Furniture and Furnishings (Fire) (Safety) (Amendment) Regulations 1988; the Toy Safety Regulations 1989, implementing EEC Directive 88/378; the Weighing Machines (Non-Automatic Weighing Machines) Regulations 1988, implementing directive 90/384; the Food

Imitations (Safety) Regulations 1989, implementing directive 87/357; and the Price Marking Regulations 1991, implementing directives 88/314 and 88/315.

Three other areas in which the EEC generated significant new regulatory pressures were:
(i) new VAT and information-gathering procedures associated with the arrival of the Single Market, enforced in the UK by HM Customs and Excise;
(ii) measures adopted as part of the reform of the Common Agricultural Policy, including 'set aside', 'cattle passports', 'plant passports', 'IACS', 'beef premium' and 'sheep quota';
(iii) 'conservation' measures taken under the Common Fisheries Policy, giving rise in the UK to the Sea Fish (Conservation) Act and many other regulatory changes affecting fishermen.

PART 1

UNCOVERING A DISASTER

by Christopher Booker

In the first days of January 1992, I was preparing my weekly column in the *Sunday Telegraph* when my eye was caught by two news items. The first reported the good fortune of Mr Roger Everdall, who farmed 1000 acres of Cambridgeshire. Ever since he began farming in 1950, despite working hard year after year, he had been in debt to the bank. But now, under a scheme devised by the EEC in Brussels to reduce the European 'grain mountain', he had been able to register the whole of his farm for 'set aside'. This meant that in 1992 he would grow nothing in his fields but weeds, for which he would be paid £80 an acre of taxpayers' money – or £80,000 a year. Mr Everdall could now look forward to the moment when, for the first time in over forty years, his bank account would be in the black – for doing virtually nothing.

The second item reported a cloud hanging over one of the best-known of Britain's traditional local industries, the shrimp fisheries of Morecambe Bay in Lancashire. Under a new EEC 'fish hygiene' directive, the fishermen had been told they would no longer be allowed to boil their shrimps in sea-water, which for centuries had given Morecambe shrimps their distinctive salty tang. Under the Brussels edict, the shrimp-men would now have to boil their shrimps in fresh water, which they would have to take out in their boats in large drums. The taste would no longer be the same.

When I read these two items, I thought how often in recent years we had been accustomed to seeing similar examples of the dream world emanating from 'Europe' floating in and out of the headlines, causing a stir for a few days and then being forgotten. Aware that the year just beginning would see the run-in to the European Single Market, due to be inaugurated on 1 January 1993, I decided that I would use my column to keep a record of the more bizarre directives and regulations coming out of Brussels over the next twelve months – and I invited readers to send in any particular 'Euro-absurdities' which caught their attention.

Immediately the letters began flowing in – and over the next few months I was able to publish many examples of the way 'EEC regulations' were seen to be changing and eroding Britain's distinctive way of life. On the Welsh borders, thatchers were no longer allowed to use 'seed aquila' reed, traditional for centuries, because it was not an EEC 'approved variety'. Charity shops were going to lose millions of pounds a year because, under EEC 'safety' rules, they were prohibited from selling second-hand toys. Slaughterhouses all over Britain were no longer allowed to use wooden-handled brooms under a 'meat hygiene' directive. Under an EEC 'bird directive' farmers would no longer be allowed to shoot magpies, rooks or pigeons raiding their crops – even though millions of songbirds a year were still being shot in France and southern Europe, without any apparent legal curbs.

During the summer of 1992, however, I found that what had begun as a fairly light-hearted exercise was turning into something more serious, calling for rather fuller investigation. Firstly, I was struck by how many letters I received from readers were reporting often long-established and successful businesses having to close down, because they could not afford to comply with 'EEC regulations'. This particularly seemed to apply to food shops, such as butchers, fishmongers and bakeries. As I began to wonder about the wider economic implications of what was going on, I was struck too by the scale of the various estimates then appearing as to the likely costs to Britain of directives still in the pipeline – such as the £8 billion it was claimed would be the cost of complying with new fire regulations posed under an EEC 'health and safety' directive.

Secondly, I began to discover a disturbing number of instances where much of the damage being caused by EEC directives was coming not from the original directives themselves but from the way they were being implemented by the civil servants in Whitehall as they drew up the regulations putting them into UK law – or even simple 'guidance' issued in Whitehall as to how the regulations should be enforced. An early instance of this was the supposed 'Brussels ban' on those charity shops selling second-hand toys. It turned out that the directive specifically exempted toys made before 1990. It was only the Department of Trade and Industry which had decided that all such toys should be included in the ban.

Thirdly, I discovered that many of the examples I was being sent of businesses being closed down by 'EEC regulations' were not in fact being hit by rules from Brussels at all. Much of the worst damage was coming from legislation that was entirely home-grown, in particular the extraordinary 'hygiene blitz' which was being carried out by local authority environmental health officers (EHOs) on hundreds and thousands of 'food businesses' – not just restaurants, pubs and shops but schools, canteens, clubs, old peoples' homes and village halls. All this, I learned, had been set in train under the government's 1990 Food Safety Act, introduced in response to the various 'hygiene scares' of the late 1980s, and in particular the hysteria over salmonella in 1988. The responsibility for all those bakeries and butchers' shops closing down, it turned out, lay not with the EC in Brussels at all – but rather more with that other 'EC', the prime mover in the 'salmonella in eggs' scare when she was junior health minister, Edwina Currie.

When I put all these points together in an article in the *Daily Telegraph* headed 'Who's That Lurking Behind The Brussels Book of Rules' on 14 September 1992, the response was astonishing.

Firstly, I had an avalanche of letters from people running businesses of all kinds, from hotels to slaughterhouses, with horror stories of being hit from all sides by a barrage of regulations, and expressing delight that at last someone in the media seemed to be waking up to what was going on.

Secondly, I learned to my surprise, my article was discussed at length by the Cabinet. What particularly struck ministers, it seemed, was my evidence that Whitehall officials were 'adding on' to the impact of Brussels directives (in one example I cited, a short directive had inspired eighty-four pages of regulations from Whitehall, while the French equivalent had only four). Partly as a result of my article, the need for 'deregulation' was chosen as a running theme for the Conservative Party Conference a few weeks later. Several ministers, including the Foreign Secretary Douglas Hurd and the Agriculture Minister John Gummer, featured it prominently in their speeches, and it was an unexpected centrepiece of the Prime Minister's own speech, with his headline-catching call to Michael 'Tarzan' Heseltine, as President of the Board of Trade, to 'put on your loincloth, get out your axe' and 'hack back the jungle of red tape'.

A third form of response, which in some ways I found most interesting of all, was a small group of letters from people whom one could call 'experts', such as a senior consultant to the meat trade, and a microbiologist. They put the point with considerable authority that what I had got into was not just a case of regulation run riot. What was really scandalous about so much that was going on, particularly in the name of 'hygiene', was that it was scientifically and technically so flawed. In practical terms, it was simply not addressing the problems it was supposed to be solving. A particularly glaring example, as meat industry consultant Don Bennett explained, was the chaos engulfing the meat trade, as a result of the way the Ministry of Agriculture, Fisheries and Food (MAFF) was implementing the EEC's meat hygiene directive. Hundreds of firms were threatened with closure, and for no benefit in terms of giving the consumer 'safer meat' at all. If anything, the opposite was true. It was, in effect, taking a mighty sledge-hammer to miss a nut.

One of the first of these experts to contact me was a 'food safety consultant' living in Yorkshire, Richard North, who sent me a long letter making this general point in a way I found so powerful that I immediately rang him up. He turned out to be a former EHO who had played a leading part in the heroic rearguard action of the egg trade to defend itself following the salmonella hysteria in 1988, in particular against the regulatory onslaught launched against the egg producers by officials of MAFF, which forced 5000 egg producers out of business. But North's concerns ran much wider than the egg industry. He was working on a doctoral thesis at Leeds Metropolitan University on the science of food-poisoning. As a former EHO, he was appalled at the way the 'hygiene blitz' waged by EHOs on food businesses had got completely out of hand, another perfect example of the sledgehammer missing the nut. But he was also profoundly alarmed by the way Britain's regulatory system seemed to be going off the rails in so many other directions. And as we talked of some of the wider issues involved, I could see that, with his technical expertise and knowledge of regulatory law, he was an ideal partner with whom to carry out a much more thorough-going investigation into the whole picture. I suggested therefore that we should work together on a book.

*   *   *

One of the first things we needed to do was to build up a much more detailed picture of just where this avalanche of regulation was coming from. In November 1992 therefore I wrote another article in the *Daily Telegraph*, headed 'What Tarzan Will Hack Back This Jungle of Bureaucracy?', appealing to readers to send in as many examples of misplaced regulation as possible. I here outlined the first of the analytical frameworks we were to devise in order to understand more clearly what was happening. This was what we called the 'six point sequence' to identify each of the main points at which the machine was going off the rails.

1. *The EEC factor*

Firstly there was the 'EEC factor', the barrage of directives from Brussels, which in the first eighteen months had been reaching a peak, with all the legislation required to create the dream of the Single Market by 1 January 1993. In addition there was a further spate of regulations and decisions from the EEC concerned with reforms of the Common Agricultural Policy (CAP) and the Commons Fisheries Policy (CFP).

2. *The Whitehall effect*

Next there was the 'Whitehall effect', the way in which UK officials so often added on new requirements to the original directives when they came to 'transpose' them into the regulations which made them into UK law, making their impact on Britain's businesses so much more damaging. This had to be contrasted with the much more relaxed approach of other

EEC countries when they came to implement and enforce the same directives.

3. Made in Britain

Then there was all the new regulatory law which was entirely home-grown and which, although it was often casually blamed on the EEC, had nothing to do with Brussels at all. This included many of the regulations having the most devastating impact, such as those brought in under the Food Safety Act 1990, the Children Act 1989 and the Community Care Act 1990.

4. Guidance enforced as law

Something which became such a significant part of the problem that it merited a separate category was the way in which 'guidance' notes issued by Whitehall to give assistance in understanding and enforcing the new regulations often went much further than the terms of the regulations themselves – and were then cited and enforced as if they were legal requirements. In many instances, as we were beginning to discover, this was doing as much damage as the regulations themselves, even leading to the closure of businesses because they were unable to comply with demands which went beyond the law.

5. Overzealous enforcement

One of the greatest problems of all, it had become clear, lay in a dramatic change which had come over the attitude of many officials directly responsible for the enforcement of regulations on the ground, such as EHOs, safety and pollution inspectors, trading standards officers and social workers. It was not just that, in many cases, these officials had been armed by recent legislation with new powers (such as those given to EHOs under the Food Safety Act, to close down food businesses without prior reference to a magistrate). A new regulatory ethos had grown up, particularly obvious in such fields as hygiene, safety and environmental protection, firing the officials with an almost puritanical zeal as to the importance of the cause they were serving. It was this which in so many cases was leading them to adopt a newly aggressive and confrontational attitude towards the people and businesses with whom they were dealing, treating even the most recognize as 'the climate of fear and confusion'. So great and found zeal which was leading the enforcers so often to part company with normal civility and common sense, even to disregard the law.

6. *The Climate of Fear and Confusion*

As a result of all this, there had arisen what we came to recognize as 'the climate of fear and confusion'. So great and seemingly so arbitrary were the powers of the enforcing officials, and so bewildering was the array of new regulations, that people had become too terrified to challenge the officials or to question their demands. When it was so difficult for them to know any longer what the law actually required (sometimes, as we will see, it was not even available to be consulted), they had become helpless victims – a situation which many officials were only too eager to exploit, by passing off 'advice' as legal 'requirements' and by making demands, backed up by the shadowy threat of legal action, which defied all practicality and reason.

When I set out something of this analysis in my *Daily Telegraph* article, the response from readers was even more remarkable than that to my article two months earlier. Some 600 letters poured in, the majority from people running every conceivable kind of business, from scrap metal yards and engineering firms to multiple grocers, from fish merchants to electronics companies, from the owners of restaurants to school headmasters, from proprietors of old peoples' homes to ships' chandlers, from dairy farmers and cheesemakers to a lady who bred tortoises in Surrey. And what came across loud and clear from all the stories they had to tell, and the mass of detailed evidence they gave, was that the regulatory onslaught which had fallen on Britain was much more wide-spread and was having a far more devastating impact than anyone had imagined. Both in human terms, of the nightmare into which it had plunged so many people's lives, and in terms of the financial costs it imposed, it was clear that the crisis of misplaced regulation was rapidly turning into a real national disaster.

*   *   *

One of the more curious features of this crisis was the way it seemed to have crept up on Britain unawares. Although it was now quite seriously affecting millions of people, it was still attracting remarkably little attention from the media. Certainly, the press was happy to highlight individual instances of 'Euro-lunacies'. As the cuttings I was sent by readers showed, local papers all over the country frequently reported the closure of long-established firms and shops because of 'EEC regulations'. But coverage of such things tended to remain remarkably superficial. And few attempts were made to see all the countless separate examples as being manifestations of the same underlying disaster. It was as if it was happening in so many directions at once that the press and television had not yet found any way of identifying it as a single, general story – and much of it simply went unreported.

Another theme of these letters was the futility of trying to raise the matter with politicians. Many of my correspondents had written to their MPs about their particular problems, and had eventually received copies of anodyne letters from ministers (written by civil servants on the ministerial word processor), blandly assuring them that their enquiry had been carefully considered, but that the regulations in question had been introduced for very good reasons and, in effect, that all was for the best in the best of all possible worlds. 'I hope you find this helpful', as the word processors almost invariably concluded their letters.

Indeed, one of the mysteries of the whole story was just how ignorant even ministers seemed to be about what was going on, even though in theory it was they who were responsible for the explosion of regulations in the first place. In the House of Commons on 24 November 1992, just ten days after my article, Douglas Hurd referred to 'cases where officials in Whitehall take decisions made in Brussels and carry them through in excessive detail':

> That is known in the jargon as 'Bookerism', after the journalist who identified the ill. Christopher Booker is strongly against the European Community, but being an honest journalist he has spotted that much of the regulation is derived not from the Community but from the itch of Whitehall to insert its own bureaucratic instincts into the process.

Certainly it was flattering to be referred to by the Foreign Secretary in this way. But what was really startling was that, in a year when he had been preoccupied with Europe almost to the exclusion of everything else (on 7 February he had signed the Maastricht Treaty and in July Britain had begun its six-month presidency of the Council of Ministers), Mr

Hurd should only now have been discovering what Britain's civil servants had been doing to the edicts of Brussels, when for many industries in Britain this was already promoting such a crisis that firms were wondering if they could survive.

As Richard North and I endlessly discussed and analysed the immense disaster we were uncovering – and more information was now coming in all the time from readers of my regular *Sunday Telegraph* column – we were beginning to evolve some general conclusions about the nature of the phenomenon we were investigating.

One thing which particularly struck us was that wherever we looked, and whatever type of activity we were considering, we found the great engine of bureaucracy and its myriad officials behaving in the same, identifiable ways, operating to the same mindset, using the same jargon, causing the same problems, making the same mistakes. It was as if we were always looking at the same enormous, blundering monster which, although it had many heads, was always in the end the same recognizable animal. We began automatically to draw a distinction between the 'world of the monster' and the 'real world', where millions of people were trying to get on with their lives, run their businesses, earn their living in, on the whole, a responsible, enterprising manner. Yet wherever the monster impinged on the real world, it invariably had the same effect. It threw out clouds of deadening jargon; it tied people up in absurd paperwork and form-filling; it made ridiculous demands; it asserted its power in a blind, wilful way; it crushed enterprise and independence; at worst, it turned far too many of those who fell under its sway into nothing more than uncomprehending and often fearful victims.

Of course, there is nothing new about bureaucracy and the power of officialdom. Bureaucrats have been an inseparable part of civilization since the days of Hammurabi, or the ancient Chinese empire. In our own time we recall such hey-days of bureaucracy as the period after the Second World War, when red tape and rationing, official 'snoopers' and the need to have permits and licences for everything were synonymous with an age when 'the man from Whitehall knows best'.

So what was new about this regulatory disaster we were uncovering in 1992? What was it that distinguished this latest manifestation of the bureaucratic monster from all those which had gone before?

Something which particularly marks out the monster in our own day is the way in which it has become particularly active in certain areas of life, which give it a special evangelical charge, a conviction that almost whatever it does is justified, because it is serving some cause so righteous that it cannot be morally questioned. North and I singled out four of these in particular, which we came to call the 'shibboleths'.

The first is 'hygiene', the belief that nothing is more important than a world in which all food is safe for 'consumers' to eat, prepared in clean, sanitized surroundings.

The second is 'safety', under which everything must be checked and double-checked to make sure no one is ever 'at risk' in any way, whether at their 'workplace' or on some form of transport or while enjoying their 'leisure'.

The third is 'environmental protection', by which every measure must be taken to ensure that the environment – air, water and soil – is not polluted.

The fourth is what may be called the institutionalized promotion of 'caring', particularly for young children and the old.

Who could possibly argue against the desirability of all those things? Certainly, if one looks at the legislation of recent years, it is remarkable how much of it has been dedicated by politicians and officials to achieving these ends, often in response to some scare or genuine disaster which has stoked up calls for 'the government to act' in the first place. The Food Safety Act appeared in 1990 in response to the salmonella, listeria and other 'hygiene' scares of the late 1980s, and this was only one of a welter of new 'hygiene' measures to appear over the next few years, such as the regulations implementing various EEC directives on the meat, poultry, fish and game trades. There was a similar deluge of new 'safety' regulations, ranging from the Electricity at Work Regulations 1989 to the six new sets of regulations implementing EEC directives on health and safety at work which came into force on 1 January 1993. Another instance, following the sinkings of the *Herald of Free Enterprise* and the *Marchioness* in the late 1980s, was the obsession with regulating the safety of almost anything that floats, from fishing boats to paddle steamers. The growing environmental concerns of the 1970s and 1980s produced no fewer than forty-eight EEC directives related to water quality (which in 1993 it was estimated were going to cost the UK alone some £45 billion to implement); while fears of global warming and depletion of the ozone layer were among the factors giving rise to the huge 240-page Environmental Protection Act 1990, which was to spawn thousands of pages of subsidiary regulations over the years that followed. The Children Act 1989 was a response to the various scandals over child abuse, both real and imaginary, from Cleveland on; while similar headline-making cases involving abuse of the elderly in retirement homes helped give rise to the Community Care Act of 1990.

Certainly, all these issues were capable of generating the most intense moralistic fervour, at the thought of humans being put 'at risk' in an unhygienic, unsafe, polluted, uncaring world. And the solution demanded by the ethos of our time has been to call for the state to intervene, to wage war on such undoubted evils with all the regulatory power that might seem necessary.

Yet the more we examined how all this deluge of regulation was working in practice, nothing became more striking than the huge gulf which had opened up between theory and reality. Again and again, as we shall see in this book, the frenzy of regulatory activity intended to promote each of these worthy causes was not properly targeted at genuine risks or problems at all. It had simply become the acting out of an obsessional ritual. This was exemplified in what we came to call the 'checklist mentality' which dominated so much regulatory enforcement. Young and inexperienced EHOs, for instance, would march into responsibly run, successful food businesses, reeling off all the points they had been told to look out for at their colleges or seminars. They would demand that thousands of pounds be spent on new 'floors, walls and ceilings', or order the replacement of anything made from wood, from chopping blocks and shelves, to rolling pins and wooden-handled brooms. Yet so preoccupied with their 'checklists' were they that when it came to identifying anything which might pose a genuine hygiene risk, their lack of practical experience would often lead them to overlook it altogether. Between 1991 and 1993, as the 'hygiene blitz' launched by the EHOs on Britain's food-handling premises under the Food Safety Act reached its height, the number of annual inspections soared from around 150,000 to 419,000. The demands they made in the name of 'hygiene' cost, in total, several billion pounds. Many businesses simply could not afford to comply, and closed down altogether.

All this had initially been set in train by the government's desire to be seen to be 'doing something' about the rapid rise in salmonella food-poisoning. Yet so hopelessly mismatched was the response to the problem that, during the very period when the 'blitz' was at its height, between the beginning of 1992 and the middle of 1993, the salmonella food-poisoning figures actually registered an increase of sixty-four per cent, their fastest rise in history.

The same 'sledgehammer to miss a nut' principle applied to much of the 'safety blitz' being carried out at the same time by a whole range of officials, from EHOs and Health and Safety Executive (HSE) inspectors, to those of the Department of Transport's Fishing Vessel Survey Department. It applied to the vast quantity of new environmental legislation, which imposed enormously costly new standards and procedures on millions of businesses, in the name of curbing often relatively trivial quantities of air, land and water 'pollution' – while most of the country's major polluting activities continued wholly or largely unaffected. It applied to often bizarrely onerous demands imposed by young social workers on privately owned nursery schools and old peoples' homes, forcing thousands to close – for reasons which had nothing to do with genuine care for children or the elderly, the very people in whose interests the whole exercise was supposedly being carried out.

Indeed in many instances we were finding that the pursuit of the 'shibboleths' was just empty ritual, achieving nothing of value. Measures intended to promote 'hygiene' were so detached from any practical understanding of hygiene that they were even producing food which was less safe to eat. The obsessive enforcement of 'safety' measures was actually making the world more dangerous. Measures taken to 'protect the environment' were in many respects tending to increase pollution rather than to diminish it. Those intended to promote proper 'caring' for the young and old ended up by causing them to suffer.

What we were looking at, in short, was a regulatory monster which had run so much out of control that, in many instances, it was producing results precisely the opposite of those intended.

*　　*　　*

Once we had begun to identify the principle whereby the net effect of regulatory activity was *not* to solve the problems at which it was directed, we could see how it applied to a startling degree to every area of life in which the new explosion of regulation was taking place.

Another area, for instance, so important that it really qualified as a fifth 'shibboleth', was the god of 'consumer protection'. A good many letters I was receiving came from those who had suffered under the cumbersome regulatory regimes set up by the Financial Services Act 1986. Bodies such as FIMBRA, LAUTRO, IMRO and the Law Society had been empowered to regulate any business which looked after customers' financial affairs, from insurance companies and financial consultants to solicitors and accountants. This involved not only costly inspections, but a huge increase in paperwork and time-consuming procedures, all of which was adding hundreds of millions of pounds to the annual cost of insurance policies and professional fees. The purpose of all this was to 'protect the consumer' against fraud and misappropriation. Yet, as was widely pointed out, the years since the new system had been created saw some of the biggest financial frauds in history, such as the Barlow Clowes and Maxwell cases. The number of cases of solicitors misappropriating clients' funds broke all records. The net effect of the new system had been only to impose substantial burdens on responsible firms, at a cost which inevitably had to be passed on to the 'consumer', while providing no protection at all against wrongdoers determined to break the rules.

In the pages which follow we shall see other examples of where regulation intended to serve the interests of 'consumers' produced many remarkable anomalies. Not least of these was the way a succession of EEC directives on things such as 'price marking' and 'non-automatic weighing machines' inspired trading standards officials to vie with the 'hygiene police' in the zeal they showed in enforcing the new regulations on thousands of small businesses.

Perhaps the most glaring instances of how regulatory activity ended up achieving results the reverse of those intended, however, came from those supreme examples of the EEC's 'Euro-planning' in action, the Common Fisheries Policy, the Common Agricultural Policy and the Single Market. We shall see in this book several instances of how the first of these, in 1992 and 1993, led the British fishing industry to the worst crisis in its history. Supposedly this was in the name of 'conserving dwindling fish stocks' round Europe's shores. Yet the most obvious immediate effect of the policy was simply that millions of tons of fish were having to be dumped dead back into the sea, or were being landed illegally as 'black' fish, making a complete mockery of 'conservation'. In the longer term, it seemed that thousands of British fishermen would be forced out of business, simply to be replaced by those of other EEC countries which were more relaxed about enforcing the so-called 'conservation' policies.

Similarly, we shall see some of the bizarre consequences of attempting to 'reform' the CAP, intended to curb fraud and to reduce huge surpluses – such as the beef and grain mountains – which had only been created by lavish subsidies in the first place. Not only in 1992 and 1993 did these enmesh Britain's farmers in an ever-growing nightmare of bureaucracy and form-filling – from 'set aside' to 'cattle passports'. They did nothing to cut down the surpluses, and only encouraged opportunities for fraud.

Finally, we shall see how empty in practice was the dream behind that main reason why 1992 and 1993 produced such a dramatic increase in the impact of Euro-legislation on Britain's businesses, the arrival on 1 January 1993 of the supposed Single Market. Despite no fewer than 218 separate directives designed to 'harmonize' economic activity throughout the EEC, it soon became clear that in many respects the 'level playing field' was as far away as ever, as other states continued to protect their own national interests or ignored the directives altogether. While for many firms in Britain the only consequence of this drive to 'liberalize' trade was the huge new burden of bureaucracy it imposed on them, as they battled to comply with a barrage of new requirements, ranging from 'Intrastat' returns to 'Procurement Directives'.

* * *

In one respect, as North and I attempted to build up a comprehensive picture of the tidal wave of regulation which was hitting Britain from all sides, we were in an unusually privileged position. Because of the unrelenting flow of letters I was receiving from readers of the Sunday and Daily Telegraphs – by the summer of 1993 the total had passed 6000, many from people running every kind of business – we could see just where the impact of misconceived regulation was creating most havoc and throwing up the most obvious anomalies. In addition to this, North was in continual contact with hundreds of businesses in two of the trades which were being hardest hit, through his role as technical adviser to the United Kingdom Egg Producers' Association and the Quality Meat and Livestock Alliance, representing hundreds of slaughterhouses, meat firms, auctioneers and farmers.

Our overriding purpose, as we identified the extent to which the great bureaucratic 'monster' was behaving in the same ways wherever it operated, was to produce a proper analysis of this extraordinary phenomenon, to see it in historical perspective, to understand the reasons why it had emerged in such an unprecedentedly virulent form in the early 1990s, and to put forward practical suggestions as to how excesses could be curbed and how the 'monster' could be brought back under proper control. For undoubtedly a crucial feature of the phenomenon was the way this 'monster' had become an autonomous force. At every level it was the officials who were running the show, dictating the agenda, extending their own powers in all directions. The elected politicians had become little more than pawns, rubber-stamping decisions which their officials had made for them, and finally appearing on television or in the House of Commons to defend the policies the officials had laid down.

When we came to plan our book on all this, it was apparent that our first task was to awaken readers to the sheer size and scale of the disaster we were describing. Although in one way or another many millions of people were already affected by it, the majority knew only a small part of the picture as it related to their own type of business. Farmers, for instance, knew little of the problems faced by fishermen, even though in both cases they were coming from the same source, MAFF. Scrap metal dealers were appalled by the difficulties they faced from regulations brought in under the Environmental Protection Act, but were not aware that the chemical industry was faced with a similar crisis by different regulations introduced under another part of the same Act.

When we began writing, therefore, we decided to begin with a series of individual case studies. Initially, this was intended to be only a curtain-raiser to the more serious analysis which was to form the rest of our book. But as one story after another, of the thousands we had available, demanded inclusion, and the cumulative effect built up, we eventually decided to publish this chapter separately as a book in its own right. At an opportune moment, I ran into my old friend and colleague, the cartoonist William Rushton, who boomed in his high-handed fashion, 'I know you're probably thinking of writing some huge and tedious book on all this regulation nonsense. But those stories in your column every week are so good that you should simply publish them as a collection, and I will do some pictures to go with them'. We have taken him at his word. Although this is still only a curtain-raiser to the more detailed book we intend to publish in due course, here is something of the extraordinary picture of life in contemporary Britain that our investigations have revealed.

PART 2

A SLEDGEHAMMER
TO MISS A NUT

Just before the First World War, G.K. Chesterton published one of his most impassioned essays, under the title *The Mad Official*. It was inspired by a brief news item reporting how an Essex labourer and his wife had been taken to court by local health officials for neglecting their five children. Although the cottage they lived in was dirty, as were the children, the prosecution did not allege that they had been in any way mistreated. Indeed it was admitted that the children were 'exceedingly well in health'. The charge was, that if they were to fall ill, the squalor in which they lived might make their condition more 'serious'. The court's remedy for this scandal was to sentence the mother to six weeks in prison; and the report ended, 'The woman was removed crying, "Lord save me!"'

Chesterton used this story to argue that there is no more alarming sign of a society taking leave of its senses than when its officials, with the full support of the law, can do something which defies all humanity and common sense – and no one takes any notice. Everyone carries on as if nothing has happened. Yet, he wrote, 'things every bit as wild are being received in silence every day . . . for madness is a passive as well as an active state'. Working himself up to one of his finest Chestertonian flights, he continued:

There are commonwealths plainly to be distinguished here and there in history which pass from prosperity to squalor, or from glory to insignificance, or from freedom to safety, not only with silence but with serenity. The face still smiles while the limbs, literally and loathsomely, are dropping from the body. These are peoples who have lost the power of astonishment at their own actions. When they give birth to a fantastic fashion or a foolish law, they do not start or stare at the monster they have brought forth. They are grown used to their own unreason; chaos is their cosmos and the whirlwind is the breath of their nostrils. These nations are really in danger of going off their heads *en masse*; of becoming one vast vision of imbecility, with toppling cities and crazy countrysides, all dotted with industrious lunatics. One of these countries is modern England.

What, one wonders eighty years later, would Chesterton have made of the England of today? Let us tour this island to look at some of the things that were going on in the Britain of 1992 and 1993.

* * *

We start our journey down in the far south-west, in Newlyn, Cornwall, the busiest fishing port in England where Nick Howell runs a firm called British Cured Pilchards. He does £100,000 of business each year sending his fish to Italy, traditionally packed in wooden boxes lined with hessian. One day in 1992, Mr Howell is notified by MAFF that he must comply with the new Food Safety (Fisheries Products) Regulations, implementing EEC Directive 91/493, which lays down the 'health conditions for the protection and placing on the market of fish products'. To comply with the regulations, he must abandon wooden boxes and pack his pilchards in plastic containers. But it is not long before his Italian customers complain that his fish arrive ruined by mould. Mr Howell pays for a scientific analysis by Exeter University which shows that the plastic containers cause the problem, because they do not allow air circulation. To save his business – and, it must be said, with the full support of his local environmental health department – he has to defy the law, by returning to traditional wooden boxes. The problem disappears.

We thus begin, appropriately enough, with an example of how regulations imposed to promote 'hygiene' – in this case an EEC directive – could lead to the very opposite. As we shall see, the obsession with wood as being 'unhygienic' was to produce startling results all over Britain. Our next story shows how the measures intended to promote 'safety' could end up by making the world more dangerous.

A big talking point with Newlyn fishermen in 1992 and 1993 is the way they must submit their boats to regular 'safety inspections' by officials of the Department of Transport's Fishing Vessel Survey Department. The fishermen have to pay fees for these inspections of £1000, plus £65 per hour, including travelling time (in 1993, following criticism, these are dropped to £220 and £44 an hour). The officials make long lists of 'safety requirements', costing anything up to £10,000. Yet a widespread complaint is that, because most officials have little experience or knowledge of fishing boats, their demands have little to do with safety and are often based on regulations which seem designed only to be appropriate for larger vessels. For instance, Mr Robert Toms, skipper of the 32-foot *Girl Penny*, is told that he must fit an 'escape hatch' to his 'engine room' so that, in case of fire, there is an alternative exit for anyone inside. This is sensible for the QE2

– but the 'engine room' on the *Girl Penny* is a wooden deck housing so small that 'not even a baby could be squeezed inside it'. Another skipper was told that he could not go fishing one day because the inspector found only forty-nine bandages in his first-aid box instead of the required fifty. Mick Mahon of the *Betty G* says, 'They've got this great checklist of safety items they expect you to have. But if there is one thing, and only one thing that I want to know I've got on board, it's a life raft on top of my wheelhouse. And what is the one thing that doesn't appear on their list? A life raft.'

What really angers the fishermen, however, is inspectors who are so incompetent that their demands actually make fishing boats positively dangerous. In the summer of 1993, for instance, Robert Downing of the *Alida T* has a fierce argument with one official who insists that he should move his fire extinguishers from the wheelhouse to the engine room. In vain does he protest that, if fire broke out in the engine, they might be impossible to reach. Sure enough, a few weeks later, this is exactly what happens. The *Alida T* is six miles offshore when the engine catches fire and pours out smoke. The four-man crew cannot reach the extinguishers, so the blaze catches hold so badly that a major air and sea rescue operation has to be mounted to snatch the four men to safety. Faced with a repair bill running into tens of thousands of pounds, for damage which need not have happened, Mr Downing is then told he will not be allowed to return to sea until he has paid another £220 plus £44 an hour for a new 'safety inspection'. He expresses the hope that officials will not send the same inspector. The water in Newlyn harbour is pretty deep.

*　　*　　*

In Penzance, George Leggett has for years been selling ice-cream from a barrow attached to a bicycle. For the right to stop at the roadside he has to pay 'rent' to Penwith Council, which has gradually been creeping up. In 1992, this amounts in the summer season to nearly £200 a month. But in 1993, council officials decide to raise this by a further 300 per cent, to £750 a month. Halfway through the summer, with his takings reduced by bad weather, Mr Leggett has paid £1700 rent to the council, almost all his income. When he rings up the neighbouring Truro Council to ask what they charge, he is told 'not more than £350 a year'. He therefore informs Penwith officials that he will no longer pay rent. He wants to be taken to court for non-payment because he see this as the only way of getting arbitration on the 'uncaring, heartless and money-grabbing' demands of the officials, which will soon drive him out of business.

*   *   *

Under an EEC directive, as interpreted by Whitehall, high-ways authorities all over Britain were having to spend up to a quarter of their entire road maintenance budgets simply on assessing all bridges in their areas to see whether they were fit to carry forty-tonne lorries. Preliminary estimates of how much it would cost to strengthen the bridges ranged from between £2 and £3 billion. As in this example, many bridges were on roads so minor that it was unlikely a forty-tonne truck would ever venture down them.

Residents of the tiny village of Porthcothan are baffled by Cornwall County Council's plans to demolish a handsome 100-year-old stone bridge over a small river running down through sand dunes to the sea nearby. Council officials say they have to replace it under the Department of Transport's Bridge Strengthening and Assessment Programme. The aim is to ensure that all bridges on classified roads in the UK can take forty-tonne lorries by 1999 – to comply with EEC

Directive 85/3 'on the weights, dimensions and certain other technical characteristics of certain road vehicles'. Residents firstly observe that it is extremely unlikely that the driver of any forty-tonne truck would be foolish enough to bring his vehicle down the narrow, twisting B-road leading to the bridge. Secondly, when they commission a professional assessment of the bridge's strength, to an established D.o.T procedure, the steel-reinforced bridge is found to be capable of carrying 'not just one forty-tonne lorry but another placed on top of it'. Thirdly, it appears that the council highways department has not even carried out the D.o.T procedure itself, before deciding to spend tens of thousands of pounds on replacing the bridge. But when the residents challenge the council as to why the replacement is therefore necessary, an official replies that since the money to enable Cornwall to comply with the EEC directive on lorry weights has been made available by the D.o.T, it would be a pity not to spend it – and cheerfully confesses that the council had recently spent some of the money on 'replacing a footbridge in Falmouth'.

*   *   *

This is our first item on the disaster the EEC's Common Fisheries Policy was bringing to Britain's fishermen – and an example of how the UK was getting the worst possible deal from being 'in Europe'.

One evening in March 1993, fishermen of Padstow along the north coast of Cornwall look out to where, six to eight miles offshore, the sea is 'lit up like a city' by dozens of French boats fishing for cod. The Cornishmen have to stay on shore because they have already caught their 'quota' of cod allowed under the EEC's CFP. Under Brussels rules, rigorously enforced by MAFF fisheries inspectors, they are only allowed to catch 1,750 tonnes of cod in the waters around the south-western end of Britain. The French are allocated 18,000 tonnes, more than ten times as much. What particularly angers the Cornishmen, however, is the knowledge that these waters had recently been solely British. In 1972, as part of the price paid for our admission to the Common Market, Edward Heath agreed that British waters, containing eighty per cent of all western European fish stocks, could be regarded as a 'common European resource'. Under the CFP, adopted at the first Maastricht summit in 1983, each country was allowed a 'quota' for each species. This meant that, having given away eighty per cent of the total fish stocks, Britain received back only thirty per cent; in terms of value under allocations for each species, only twelve per cent. Now, not only are Cornish fishermen prevented from earning a living, having to stay at home watching the French boats fishing in what had once been their waters. When they turn on the television news, they see French fishermen running riot in ports and markets destroying millions of pounds worth of fish exported to France from Britain – in protest against a general collapse in prices because of a glut of cod.

*   *   *

In April 1993, a new bureaucratic body appeared, the Child Support Agency, set up under the Child Support Act 1991 with 4700 officials, to assess, enforce and collect payments for child maintenance from absent fathers. Its powers were extensive, ranging from the right to force employers to collect the money by docking their employees' wages, to the power to overrule the financial arrangements agreed by courts in divorce settlements. It was not long before the officials of the CSA showed they were just as capable as others of wielding their new sledgehammer to miss the nut.

In Plymouth, Devon, in the summer of 1993, Mrs Sue Collins, a young mother of three, receives a letter to say she will shortly be visited by an inspector of the Child Support Agency. When she rings the local office of the Department of Social Security to ask what the visit is about, an official explains that it is in connection with an investigation into her husband Kevin, a Ministry of Defence policeman, who in a relationship with another woman has fathered a child. Mrs Collins is horrified, and the call leads to a major confrontation with her husband, in which she says that she will have to divorce him. Only when further details are obtained does it emerge that Mr Collins is being accused of having fathered a child in the West Country, at a time when he had been a 15-year-old schoolboy living in Croydon. It turns out that the officials had only identified Mr Collins as the father because the name 'Kevin Collins' had been fed into a computer, and certain other details had seemed to match up with his. The agency eventually admits that 'a mistake was made'. An angry Mr Collins points out that the agency 'appears to find people guilty until they are proved innocent' and that the mistake nearly cost him his wife and children.

*   *   *

The National Rivers Authority (NRA), set up on the privatisation of water in 1989, had discovered a huge new source of income – worth more than £40 million a year – in charging any business which used water which 'belonged' to them because it was part of a stream or river system. The officials could be particularly imaginative in deciding what constituted a 'business'.

For thirty years children at the Stoke Gabriel Primary School, on the River Dart, have in the summer enjoyed splashing about in a tiny two-foot deep 'paddling pool'. It is filled by winter rainfall and when it needs emptying the water is carried by buckets to a nearby storm drain. In the summer of 1993 the school governors are astonished to be informed by officials of the NRA that their school is a 'business' and their paddling pool is a 'learning resource'. They must therefore pay an £1831-a-year 'discharge account' for the use of the water and for pouring it down the drain. The governors sadly conclude that the use of the pool will have to be discontinued.

* * *

Hotels were only one of the many types of small businesses which in 1992 and 1993 found themselves hit by absurd regulations from several directions at once. We shall return later to the strange story of the Electricity at Work Regulations – but this is also the first example of the ever more bizarre demands now made by EHOs as they launched into the most ferocious 'hygiene blitz' in history.

Near Kingsbridge, David and Graham Grose run the 4-star Thurlestone Hotel. Like other hotel owners all over Britain, they have been hit by such an avalanche of new bureaucratic burdens that in April 1993 their local MP, Anthony Steen, raises their case in the House of Commons. Under the new Electricity at Work Regulations, for instance, they have been told that they must now have every electrical appliance in the hotel subjected to exhaustive tests each year by a 'qualified electrician', with records kept of each test. This means not only that the television sets, trouser presses, kettles, lamps and plugs in the hotel's sixty-eight bedrooms must be examined; each of the standard lamps must be 'numbered, tested and given its own log book'. As David Grose explains, 'it will take somebody three months a year to test everything'. But what catches the headlines is the instruction given to kitchen staff by a South Hams EHO, that to make a ham and tomato

sandwich, they must use two separate knives – one for the 'cooked' produce (the ham), the other for 'raw' (the tomato). Which knife to use to cut through the finished sandwich, the EHO does not make clear.

*　　*　　*

In Teignbridge, businessman Peter Barnes has been told by a building control officer from his local council that, when putting up a two-storey office extension, he must install a lift – just in case he has a job application from a disabled person. The lift costs him £30,000. Two years later, the lift has never been used – and Mr Barnes has to pay £1000 a year for maintenance.

*　　*　　*

In Newton Abbot Hospital, it has been the custom for the local Rotary club to celebrate Christmas by serving a turkey dinner to patients on the wards. But, in 1992, EHOs from Teignbridge District Council tell them that this is an offence against food hygiene regulations. The Rotarians go round the wards serving Bucks Fizz instead.

*　　*　　*

It was not only in the field of food hygiene that EHOs were displaying their newfound zeal for putting the world to rights. 'Safety', 'environmental pollution' – there was no end to their expertise.

In Exeter, in July 1993, a young EHO arrives at the Bracken Court care home for the elderly, owned and run by Mrs Vivienne Sinkins. His attention is caught by an electric chair lift, used to move infirm residents up and down the stairs. According to Mrs Sinkins, this appears 'to fascinate him' and he spends almost an hour 'playing with it', repeatedly starting and stopping it (strictly contrary to manufacturer's instructions), placing a box in the works to see whether it will break, and finally waving the power cable repeatedly above his head (again contrary to manufacturer's instructions). The purpose of all this baffles Mrs Sinkins. Her chair lift has been manufactured and installed to the highest standards by the world's leading makers of such equipment, is regularly maintained and inspected, and has never given the slightest problem. But the young official, who admits that this is his first day at work since qualifying as an EHO, says he is 'worried' by the lift, although he cannot explain why. Next day he returns with a colleague, introduced as 'Claire', to spend a further hour on the machine. A day later he rings up Mrs Sinkins to say he is writing to her about the chair lift, and that he is still 'worried by it', although he still cannot explain why. A subsequent expert inspection by the specialist company which regularly maintains the lift shows that the power cable has suffered minor damage and will have to be replaced. It also comes to light that under the Hoists and Lifts Regulations 1968 and the Electricity at Work Regulations 1989, it is a criminal offence for anyone who is not a 'competent person', a qualified electrician, to do anything with such a chair lift except use it in the normal way, and according to the manufacturer's instructions.

*   *   *

No piece of recent legislation was to have more wide-ranging consequences for millions of businesses than the Environmental Protection Act 1990. Many of these were only coming to light in 1992 and 1993 as the thousands of pages of new regulations introduced under the Act began to come into force. Some of the most important sections of the EPA were concerned with implementing extremely rigorous standards for 'air pollution' laid down by officials in Brussels. Although

*they were widely ignored in other Member States, the zeal
with which they were beginning to be enforced in Britain was
posing a serious threat to many industries, as we shall see.
Our first example merely highlights one of the more ridiculous anomalies thrown up by this Act.*

In Okehampton, Alison Maddaford, chairman of the legislat-
ive committee of the National Association of Funeral Direc-
tors, is talking about the many consequences of the EPA for
Britain's undertakers. In accordance with an EEC directive,
this Act imposes tight controls on the substances which may
be used in making coffins which are to be burned in crematoria. But other countries, such as Spain, have not yet bothered
to implement this directive. One consequence is that, every
year, when between 200 and 300 Britons die in Spain and
are shipped over in Spanish coffins, they have, on arrival at
a British undertakers, to be 'de-coffined'. This is because there
is no proof that Spanish coffins meet the requirements of UK
regulations under the EPA which give effect to EEC Directive
84/360 on the 'combatting of air pollution from industrial
plants', as this relates to crematoria. It is, therefore, illegal
for British crematoria to burn Spanish coffins, and the corpses
have to be 're-coffined' in UK-made boxes, so that forbidden
substances do not pollute the air. However, the undertakers
then have the problem of disposing of the unwanted Spanish
coffins. 'What most do', according to another undertaker, 'is
take them out the back and put them on a bonfire' – which
under the D.o.E regulations is perfectly legal.

*　　*　　*

*Few pieces of legislation were to have more devastating conse-
quences in Britain in 1992 and 1993 than the meat hygiene
directive, which as we shall see was to spread havoc throughout the meat trade. Our first example highlights one of the*

several ways in which MAFF's implementation of this direc-
tive was to inflict suffering on thousands of animals.

In South Molton cattle market in February 1993, an angry
crowd is gathered round a cow which is bellowing with pain
after sustaining serious injury in transit. In the old days the
animal would soon have been put out of its agony. But now,
under the new Fresh Meat (Hygiene and Inspection) Regulations, introduced by MAFF to implement the EEC meat
hygiene directive, 91/497, the animal has to continue
bellowing for an hour, because it cannot be killed until its
owner has managed to summon a vet to make an ante-
mortem inspection, a licensed slaughterman to kill it and a
designated vehicle to take it away.

*   *   *

No EEC measure caused more bureaucratic chaos in Britain
than the demand imposed on farmers to fill in what one NFU
spokesman described as 'The Mother of All Forms', recording
the exact area of their fields.

Nearby in Somerset, in April 1993, two Exmoor hill farmers,
John Edwards and his son Oliver, have had to commission
the Ordnance Survey (OS) to survey every inch of their farm.
In common with nearly 300,000 other farmers, they have
been given six weeks by MAFF to fill in a complex form, with
the 'aid' of a 79-page explanatory booklet, giving the exact
cultivable area in hectares of each of their fields, to two deci-
mal places. Areas occupied by footpaths, hedges, ditches or
electricity pylons must be subtracted. This is part of a scheme
originating in Brussels known as IACS (Integrated Administration and Control System), designed to record the precise
measurements of every field in the EEC (the result will be
checked against infra-red photographs taken from space by

four satellites, two American and two French). The purpose of this new 'Domesday Book' is to catch farmers who make fraudulent subsidy claims which, according to the President of the European Commission's Court of Auditors, account for £6 billion, or more than a fifth of the EEC's entire annual expenditure under the Common Agricultural Policy of £28 billion. In Italy, for instance, in 1991, farmers claimed hundreds of millions of pounds-worth of subsidies on 4.2 million hectares of duram wheat, used for making pasta, whereas satellite photographs showed they were only in fact growing 1.9 million hectares. For several weeks in April 1993, there are extraordinary scenes all over Britain, as tens of thousands of farmers besiege OS offices to obtain the necessary large-scale maps. Queues begin forming outside some offices at 3.30 a.m., other offices remain open until midnight. Farmers have to make round-trips of up to 200 miles, only to find that even if the maps are in stock, they often do not contain the detailed information required. But for John and Oliver Edwards, and hundreds of other farmers in the more remote areas, the problem is even worse. They discover that OS has not yet mapped their farm to the required scale. Faced with dire penalties if they fail to fill their forms in properly, or on time, they must therefore hurriedly pay £800 for their own survey. Aware that farmers elsewhere in the EEC are faced with none of these problems (in France, field-areas are already recorded in the town halls, and maps have been sent out by the French agriculture ministry), John Edwards – a Conservative County Councillor – writes to Agriculture Minister John Gummer, 'this will surely prove to be the biggest fiasco MAFF has ever put its hands to'.

* * *

In south Somerset, Sir Antony Jay (one of the co-authors of 'Yes Minister') lives with his wife Jill in a house they have converted from a barn. A local building control officer tells them that a staircase they propose for the first floor is 'too steep'. To accommodate the stairs at the 'correct' angle involves knocking down a wall. Eventually, the Jays ask what would happen if, instead of making the staircase less steep, they make it steeper. The official rules that it would then no longer be a 'stairway' but a 'ladder', and gives his approval.

*   *   *

The extraordinary disaster of MAFF's new 'meat hygiene' regulations was to produce hundreds of bizarre stories – but one of the more curious features of this was the way officials began enforcing the law even before anyone knew what it was. Millions of pounds were spent on complying with 'guidance notes', which later turned out to include many items which were not required by law at all.

In the summer of 1992 Edwin Snell, the butcher in Chard, is puzzling over structural changes to his small slaughterhouse, required by MAFF if he wishes to stay in business after 1 January 1993. He is told that under the proposed new Fresh Meat (Hygiene and Inspection) Regulations, implementing EEC Directive 91/497, live animals must be brought in by one entrance and carcasses must leave via a separate exit. Since Mr Snell's premises have only one access to the nearby road, he must spend thousands of pounds building an additional road. What puzzles him is why he should spend this money, supposedly in the name of 'hygiene', when, within ten yards – the length of his existing access road – live and dead animals will pass on the main road. Even more puzzling is the fact that there is nothing whatsoever in the directive about separate site entrances and exits. The MAFF regulations have yet to be published, much less approved by parliament, so there is no way of knowing whether the works are required by the regulations. At the time he is expected to carry out the works, Mr Snell only has the MAFF 'guidance notes' issued to slaughterhouse owners, to 'assist' him in complying with the as yet unpublished regulations. Like hundreds of other abattoir owners, Mr Snell is thus being ordered to spend thousands of pounds on something which is not a legal requirement.

At Ashcott, near Glastonbury, another butcher faced with the same problem is Paul Griffiths, who owns five butchers' shops in mid Somerset. His small slaughterhouse is in an eighteenth-century building on a site with only one entrance. To comply with the unpublished regulations, he has been instructed by MAFF officials to build a new access road the other side of his slaughterhouse, and a new entrance to the building. He will not only have to get planning permission to make changes to a Grade II listed building, he must buy an adjoining field, which the owner is prepared to sell to him for £50,000.

When MAFF finally published its regulations, in September 1992, they did not contain any requirement for separate entrances or exits, or for many of the other 'requirements' that MAFF was insisting upon.

*　　*　　*

No one will ever know how many billions of pounds were spent in 1992 and 1993 to comply with the demands of EHOs as they went on their great 'hygiene' and 'safety' spree. Here is just one example – which is also another of how 'safety' measures increased risk.

Near Shepton Mallet in February 1993, one of the leading agricultural shows, the Royal Bath and West, announces a deficit for 1992 of £91,000 – its first loss in twenty years. It also announces that, to comply with 'hygiene and safety' demands made by EHOs of the local Mendip District Council during the year has cost £250,000. Now officials are making new demands, including the replacement of traditional wooden and rope fencing around the main show ring by metal crash barriers, at a cost of £30–40,000. The experience at other showgrounds is that if animals panic, these can be very dangerous, both to the animals and spectators. Whereas the traditional ring surround 'gives', so delaying the animal and allowing the crowd to scatter, the rigid, heavy metal barriers are likely to collapse suddenly under the weight of a stricken animal, crushing spectators and injuring the animal. But the EHOs are demanding these in the name of 'safety'.

*　　*　　*

A particular mania among many different types of official in 1992 was to demand that people should go on 'courses', to be instructed in anything from 'hygiene' to how to operate a petrol pump. The vast majority of these courses were babyish beyond belief, and taught those who went on them – often experienced professionals – nothing they did not know already. But they made a hefty income for those who received the fees, and as this example shows, it was therefore very advantageous that people could somehow be persuaded that such courses were mandatory.

The authorities who run the magnificent medieval Bishop's Palace in Wells, Somerset, in January 1993 send a letter advertising the success of their charity open days, staged by local charitable organizations to raise funds and recruit new members. As the outstanding example from 1992, they cite the day run by the Somerset Trust for Nature Conservation, which raised a good deal of money, not least through the sale of an array of food and drink provided by dozens of members. The letter adds that 'under the Food Safety Act 1990', anyone involved in food handling 'will need to be trained and hold the necessary Institution of Environmental Health Officers Basic Food Hygiene Certificate (the current price for the training is circa £35 per person)'. When the Somerset Trust for Nature Conservation sees this, it realizes that it cannot afford to send its army of helpers on 'food hygiene' courses at £35 a head, and reluctantly decides it must now cancel plans for another open day at the Bishop's Palace. What neither they nor the staff at the Bishop's Palace realize is that the Food Safety Act 1990 does not require anyone to go on hygiene courses. Yet it has certainly served the interests of the Institution of Environmental Health Officers (IEHO) that such a misunderstanding should have arisen. Since 1991, the IEHO has enjoyed a huge rise in its income from awarding 'hygiene certificates' to nearly a million people who have been on such courses. And it is also true that all over the country food businesses and other organizations, like the Women's Royal Voluntary Service, which runs hundreds of meals-on-wheels operations, have for some reason been led to understand that such courses are now obligatory. But the idea that there is any legal requirement is wholly imaginary.

*　　*　　*

Like building control officers, fire control officers were empowered to make expensive demands which often seemed quite arbitrary and without any practical purpose.

At Ston Easton Park, between Wells and Bath, Peter and Christine Smedley run a country house in a large eighteenth-century mansion, listed Grade 1. In 1982 when they converted the house to a hotel they were required by local fire officers to place small white stickers with red triangles on all fire doors, reading 'Fire Door Keep Shut'. In the late 1980s, a new fire officer arrived and said the white stickers were 'out

of date'. They should be replaced with larger green, diamond-shaped notices, attached to each door with two screws, reading 'Fire Door Keep Shut'. This required repainting all the doors at a cost of £2000. Now in 1993, yet another fire officer comes along and says the green notices are 'obsolete'. They must be replaced with still larger blue square signs with four screws (which damage the period doors) reading 'Fire Door Keep Shut'. While the hotel's handyman is busy in the house changing the white stickers to the green notices, his workshop outside the house burns down, at a cost of £20,000.

*   *   *

The 'safety blitz' launched by the Department of Transport on every type of passenger vessel, in the wake of the Herald of Free Enterprise *and* Marchioness *disasters of the late 1980s, here threatens a disaster of another kind.*

From Clevedon, Weston-super-Mare and other ports along the Bristol Channel in the summer of 1993, tens of thousands of passengers board the *Waverley*, one of only two surviving paddle steamers in the country. Like the smaller *Kingswear Castle*, which operates around the Thames estuary, the *Waverley* has been rescued and lovingly restored by a small army of highly professional volunteers of the Paddle Steamer Preservation Society. It has for some years been making dozens of trips each summer down the Bristol Channel and around the Clyde in Scotland. But now passengers are startled to see notices posted in the ship to say that, unless the Society can raise an astronomic sum by 1993 to pay for new 'safety requirements', the vessels will not be allowed to continue in service. But when the D.o.T applied the rules to paddle steamers, one of the safest known forms of transport (last fatal accident in 1878), it soon became clear that its inspectors were quite unfamiliar with this type of vessel. One of their first demands was for bulkheads down the middle of the *Waverley*'s engine room, which would have made it impossible to work the paddle wheels. Another was for glass in the saloon windows so thick that trapped passengers could not have broken out. It seemed that some of the demands might have been appropriate for a large cross-channel ferry like the *Herald of Free Enterprise*, others for 'an overgrown river launch' like the *Marchioness*, but were not relevant to sturdily built paddle boats. With exemplary patience, the society eventually negotiated the officials' demands down to a new emergency bilge-pumping system (in addition to the one already installed), and a mass of new lifejackets and other safety equipment (in addition to that already carried). This will cost the small charitable society £350,000. Unless it can be raised in two years, the pleasure enjoyed by hundreds of thousands of passengers will soon be a thing of the past.

*　　*　　*

In Saltford, near Bristol, George Seager is the landlord of a local pub, the Jolly Sailor. In July 1992, he is visited by an EHO of Wansdyke Council, who finds the pub's cat Jo-Jo lying on a chair in the 'restaurant area' and the landlord's dog Mickey in a basket in the bar. The EHO informs Mr Seager that these are serious breaches of hygiene regulations. He is going to serve an 'Emergency Prohibition Notice', closing down the pub until Jo-Jo the cat has been 'disposed of'. He will, however, permit Mr Seager to keep his dog.

*　　*　　*

In Trent, Dorset, in the summer of 1993, the villagers are up in arms because Charles Marion-Crawford, the landlord of their local pub the Rose and Crown, is being taken to court by West Dorset District Council on thirty-three criminal charges under the Food Safety Act 1990. In eight years, Mr Marion-

Crawford has built the pub into one of the most successful for miles around. His food has been commended by Egon Ronay and Les Routiers and his pub has never had a case of food-poisoning. The charges against him include the failure to have a nailbrush on a handbasin; having an 'unlidded rubbish bin' in the kitchen (only open because it was in use when the EHO called); and keeping 'dead flies' in a device for killing insects. The penalties for each of such 'offences' can be fines of up to £5000, and two years in prison. As one villager puts it, 'half the houses in the village have been broken into and robbed. Yet the only person we see visibly receiving the might of the law is a man earning an honest living, with a young family. Where has common sense got to?'

In August 1993, following extensive publicity given to this case in the Sunday Telegraph, *Mr Marion-Crawford arrived at Dorchester Crown Court to face his criminal prosecution, supported by a crowd of villagers. Everyone present was amazed to hear that the EHO, Mr John, had 'gone on holiday', taking the documents of the case with him. There would therefore be no case to answer. The judge gave Mr Marion-Crawford an absolute discharge.*

*　　*　　*

In Portland, just before Christmas 1992, an EHO from the South Dorset District Council informs the authorities at the local naval base that, under food hygiene regulations, they must discontinue the Royal Navy's centuries old tradition of stirring the Christmas pudding with wooden oars. Wood is no longer accepted as hygienic and they must use plastic spoons instead.

*　　*　　*

This is our first example involving those official champions of proper 'caring' for the old, the young and the infirm, the

social workers. Armed with extensive powers to remove
people physically from their homes, they did not hesitate to
use them.

Elsewhere in Dorset, on 21 January 1993, a group of social
workers led by a psychiatrist arrive at the home of an 81-year-
old retired naval officer, Captain George Symonds – formerly
Commodore-in-charge and Queen's Harbourmaster in Hong
Kong – telling his 70-year-old wife that they are going to take
away her husband, by force if necessary. In 1988, Captain
Symonds began suffering from a series of small strokes which
left him mentally impaired and, in January 1992, the Dorset
County Council Social Services Department provided his wife
with half an hour's help each evening in getting the Captain
to bed. One night in January 1993, the usual girl helper
arrives three hours earlier than usual, saying that she is going
to a party. The Captain refuses to go to bed early and becomes
'very difficult'. A few days later the doorbell rings and Mrs
Symonds sees what she calls 'the snatch squad' on her door-
step. She locks herself and her husband in the kitchen, but
the social workers threaten to break her door down and call
the police. Eventually, the Captain is taken away. When, the
next day, Mrs Symonds is allowed to see him in hospital, as
she later recalls, 'He was stuffed full of drugs and unable to
recognize me, for the first time ever. I was heartbroken.' After
an appeal to a mental health tribunal, Captain Symonds is
allowed to return home. But the social services department
will offer no more help. Mrs Symonds has to pay for private
agency staff to help put her husband to bed.

*   *   *

The arrival of the Single Market on 1 January 1993, allowing
the free movement of goods and animals across borders in
the EEC, threw up a host of anomalies. For the UK one of

the most damaging of these resulted from the reluctance of the UK government to 'harmonise' tax rates on alcohol, which meant that it now became cheaper for British citizens to import drink for personal consumption from France.

At Harnham, near Salisbury, Wiltshire, Christopher Gilbey of the Nadder Wine Company is looking, in May 1993, at quotations for supplying large quantities of champagne and wine for a wedding in July. The first, his own company's, is for £3608.80. The other, representing the cost of bringing the same amount of drink from France, is £2250. The huge difference in price is accounted for by the difference between UK and France tax rates on wine. In the UK, duty and VAT on a bottle of wine is £1.16; in France it is only 2.5p. Not surprisingly, Mr Gilbey's potential customer decides to take advantage of his new Single Market freedom, and buy his wedding drinks in France. Mr Gilbey calculates that tax discrepancies are now costing his company around £35,000 a year in lost business.

The same sort of thing is happening all over Britain in 1993, causing immense damage to the UK domestic drinks trade. The worst of this results from vast quantities of beer imported from France, where it is two-thirds cheaper. A 24-bottle pack costing £21.50 in Britain costs only £7.50 in France. Not surprisingly, huge quantities of beer are being privately imported which not only hits domestic beer sales but inflicts major damage on UK tax revenue. Similar losses result from private imports of tobacco, wine and spirits. In the autumn of 1993, it is estimated that the loss to the UK exchequer in the first year of the Single Market is likely to top £500 million.

*   *   *

Also in Wiltshire in April 1993, motorists across the Downs are startled to see a large roadside sign with the word 'Crazy' in capital letters, standing in front of a weed-covered field. The notice, erected by free-range chicken farmer Martin Pitt, reads:

> *This field is not being farmed badly.* It ought to be growing high-quality wheat especially to feed my free-range chickens. Last year the field grew enough corn to produce over 200,000 free-range eggs. Under EEC regulations it must not now be farmed – weeds must be left to grow – chickens must not use the land – what a waste! And there's another 35 acres of Lovett's Farm like it that you cannot see.

Mr Pitt is one of tens of thousands of farmers being forced to take land out of production as part of the EEC's latest scheme to reduce Europe's 'grain mountain'. In 1993, more than 1.5 million acres of UK farmland – an area the size of Lincolnshire – will be 'set aside'. This represents the highest percentage of any country in the EEC, because Britain's farmers produce more to the acre than any others and therefore are the most efficient. Experts predict that, within a few years under the Brussels rules, the area of Britain's arable land forcibly set aside to grow weeds could rise to as high as thirty per cent, or nearly one third of all the crop-growing land in the country.

*   *   *

One of the strangest features of the Environmental Protection Act 1990 was the way it put an end to every kind of beneficial 'recycling', by imposing tight controls on the disposal of anything which could conceivably be described as 'waste'. Here was one particularly absurd example.

In Pewsey, the huntsman of the local Tedworth Hunt has for some years been calling each weekend at Marshall's Bakery

to collect leftover bread and cakes to feed to his hounds. But as from 1 April 1993, this must stop. Under the new Waste Management Regulations introduced under the Environmental Protection Act 1990, the leftovers must be classified as 'controlled waste'. They can only be transported by someone with a Waste Carrier's License costing £95, from the county Waste Regulation Authority, and given to someone with a licence to receive waste, at a cost of £1800. The bread and cakes are now removed as part of the bakery's regular rubbish collection, for burial in a properly licensed tip.

*   *   *

In Trowbridge, Mr Philip Gilbert, who runs Aaron Taxis, receives a solicitor's letter from his local water company, Wessex Water Services, stating that he owes them £223.04 and threatening action if he does not pay up immediately. Mr Gilbert is puzzled. His tiny premises contain neither a tap nor a lavatory. What 'services' is he being charged for? Apparently, the water company has discovered that Mr Gilbert sometimes uses the lavatory of the shop next door and occasionally fills a kettle from its tap. Mr Harry Morgan, an official of Wessex Water explains, 'He uses water from the adjoining premises. He uses toilets in the adjacent premises. Therefore he ought to pay' (even though the shop next door has already paid).

*   *   *

A choice example of the extra burdens laid upon business by the joys of belonging to the Single Market – usually, as in this case, serving no useful purpose whatsoever.

In Swindon, a small company called Colecton Research has for some time been supplying Irish farmers with a sulphur-based ointment called 'Golden Udder', for treating mastitis in cows. The firm is now told that, under EEC Regulation 90/2377, because no veterinary product containing sulphur has been licensed in Ireland before 1992, Colecton will have to provide the European Commission's veterinary directorate with scientific evidence that sulphur is a 'safe' product. He will also have to circulate the evidence to the relevant departments of each of the twelve member-state governments, and show proof that the evidence has been received. Colecton's thesis on sulphur eventually runs to 280 pages, and costs the firm several thousand pounds to compile. It is sent out to the twelve governments: the reply received from Luxembourg states, 'These parts are not requested by our administration. We have destroyed them'.

*   *   *

Another group of enforcement officials for whom Britain's membership of the EEC was providing a field day were the trading standards officers (TSOs). In 1992 and 1993 they seemed almost to be outvying the EHOs in their zeal, as they took hundreds of firms to court for offences under the UK regulations intended to implement EEC directives on 'toy safety', 'consumer protection' and 'price marking'. There was a time when we might have looked to the courts to curb some of the officials' wilder excesses. But one of the more disturbing trends of recent years, particularly as administrative law has become more technical and removed from everyday reality, has been the increasing tendency of magistrates and judges to view the officials as 'experts', whose views should be upheld regardless of common sense. Here is a particularly ludicrous example.

In Ringwood, Acorn Hobbycraft Ltd makes model kits which are sold all over the country through such outlets as W.H. Smith and Woolworths. The kits include an ordinary wire pipe-cleaner, 260 million of which have been sold in Britain in thirteen years, for the craft market. In December 1992, the company is taken to court by TSOs of Barking and Dagenham Council for offences against the Toy Safety Regulations, implementing EEC Directive 88/378 on 'the approximation of laws of the Member States concerning the safety of toys'. The officials allege that children using the kit might poke the pipe-cleaner into their eyes, thus causing them serious injury. To support their case, they have paid several thousands of pounds for experiments to be carried out involving poking pipe-cleaners into the eye of a dead pig. The magistrates reject their case and order the council to pay £30,000 compensation to the company for loss of sales. The officials appeal against this order and, in October 1993, after a hearing which lasts four days and involves two QCs, Judge Peter Fanner upholds their appeal. The pipe-cleaners are ruled to be illegal, and the total costs to the company of the TSOs zeal are estimated at 'more than £250,000'. The TSOs themselves comment that it has been 'a historic victory'.

* * *

This was a particularly tragic case of the havoc created by MAFF's efforts to force British businesses into a Single Market straitjacket, even before the relevant EEC directives had been agreed. In this instance the MAFF officials were so eager to enforce their 'guidance', even though it had no force in law, that a highly successful business was forced to close down. But there was no regret from a supposedly Conservative minister, who happily endorsed his officials' appalling blunder.

In the New Forest, Mr Andrew Fairweather sits looking out at a collection of abandoned sheds. Here during the 1980s he had built up the second-largest quail farm in Britain, selling

200,000 dressed birds a year to wholesalers from Plymouth to Glasgow. But one day in 1991, Mr Fairweather received from the Ministry of Agriculture a booklet entitled 'Food Sense - 1992 and you', on how to compete in the Single Market. He opened it without any sense of foreboding, to discover that, although quail had previously been regarded as 'game', they were now officially 'poultry', and therefore came under a proposed new EEC Poultry Meat Hygiene Directive. When he read through the twenty pages of requirements, Mr Fairweather gradually realized that his quail farm was now being treated as if it was a large-scale poultry processor – and that to stay in business would involve him in major rebuilding works and other changes which would cost him hundreds of thousands of pounds, more than his entire annual turnover. Among the lesser requirements, he would have to install showers so that he and his six employees could wash every time they moved from one shed to another, which would be many times a day. Mr Fairweather attempted to contact MAFF to discuss his problem, but despite many months of telephoning he could not find any official who 'showed any signs of understanding my position'. Furthermore, he was also being told by his customers that, unless he complied with the new regulations, they would no longer be permitted to buy birds from him. Finally, he had to accept that there was no way he could afford to stay in business and, in December 1991, he closed down the Long Reach Quail Farm, putting six people on the dole. Yet it later turns out that the EEC poultry hygiene directive in question was not even issued until December 1992, a full year after the farm closed – and the regulations bringing the directive into UK law still had not been published six months after that. Thus, Mr Fairweather had been told that it was illegal for him to stay in business unless he complied with regulations which, eighteen months later, had still not become law. When, early in 1993, this extraordinary situation is raised with MAFF, Food Minister Nicholas Soames merely replies that the closure has been made necessary by EEC legislation. Nevertheless, he adds, it may be 'helpful' to know that, under a subsequent directive, quail are no longer classified as 'poultry' but have again been reinstated as game.

* * *

Many times in the course of our investigations we came across people who seemed to have been singled out by the officials for a whole series of bureaucratic blows, all dealt at much the same time. Here is a particularly surreal example – culminating in the strange affair of 'the MAFF Official and the brick'.

Near Fordingbridge, also in the New Forest, Freda Williams runs the Dreamskerry quarantine cattery, where cats brought into Britain from abroad can be looked after during their six-month period of enforced separation. The cattery was established in 1982 at the suggestion of the Ministry of Agriculture when Miss Williams unexpectedly had to return from America with seventeen pedigree Manx cats. It was built under ministry supervision, had been regularly inspected without any problems, and the cats were visited each day by a MAFF-appointed vet. But in the autumn of 1992, Miss Williams receives two visits from a new MAFF inspector, Mr Gidman. In February 1993, she is informed by his superior, Mr Widden, that seventeen 'deficiencies' have been found in her premises and that all licences to owners to send their cats to Dreamskerry have been suspended. She is at the same time told that she faces criminal prosecution on ten counts in the local courts.

It turns out that MAFF has already been in contact with the cat owners who have booked in animals from all over the

world, to tell them that they cannot send their animals to Dreamskerry. In Chicago, one couple who have sold their home are about to fly to England; they are up all night wondering what to do next. Another owner whose cat is about to travel to England is out of communication on a Saudi oil rig. Two more cats are already being carried across Outer Mongolia on a yak, at the start of a five-day journey to England. These are problems enough but what startles Miss Williams even more is that many of the 'deficiencies' in her premises appear to be imaginary, relating to such items as the claimed absence of bolts on doors, or the lack of a sign on her gate, all of which have in fact been in place ever since the cattery was built in 1982. The trivial remaining problems are quickly rectified, and within a short time the cat owners are notified that Dreamskerry is open for business after all.

But the story is not over yet. In May 1993, another official, Mr Gibbons, arrives from the MAFF veterinary division at Tolworth Towers in Surbiton to confirm that all is now in order. Only one thing it seems is still troubling him and his colleagues – a window in her house overlooking the quarantine pens, containing several panes of reinforced glass, installed under MAFF supervision in 1982, so that Miss Williams could keep an eye on the cats from her living room. Mr Gibbons announces that he has brought a brick in his car and wishes to throw it at the glass to see if it is strong enough to stop a cat escaping through it. After some discussion as to whether this is really the most sensible way to test the glass, Mr Gibbons proposes instead that he should hit the panes with a large piece of wood. After further discussions, Gibbons admits that he and his MAFF colleagues had originally contemplated throwing a dead cat at the glass and he now suggests that the most suitable equivalent would be a 5lb joint of meat to throw at the window, which he proposes to acquire. Discussion then turns on what percentage of the joint should be flesh or bone. Finally, Miss Williams asks whether it might not be a better idea to contact the manufacturer of the glass to ask for technical specifications. Mr Gibbons says that he will have to refer to Tolworth to see whether this suggestion is 'acceptable'. A few days later, Miss Williams is notified that it is. Everything is now in order except that Miss Williams still faces adjourned charges in the local magistrates' court, under the ten summonses issued on the same day in February when she was told that her cattery was being closed down.

*　　*　　*

During the same months that she was being persecuted by MAFF, Miss Williams was also having to face the closing stages of a bizarre legal battle with her local council, which seems to exemplify the conflict between two quite different worlds – one representing the way of English rural life in days gone by, the other the Brave New World of the modern official.

In the middle of Fordingbridge on 25 August, a small angry crowd gathers to watch a 4′ 9″ woman, Liz Hennell, trying to stop a burly bailiff for New Forest District Council forcibly removing three elderly horses from a field in the middle of the town. The five-acre field has been home to the horses, owned by Miss Freda Williams, all their lives. Two are twenty-five years old, and a vet has advised that one, a small pony called Comanche, has a serious heart condition and should not be moved in a horse box. But despite an offer from Miss Hennell, a friend of Miss Williams, to walk the horses through the town later in the day when the streets are quieter, council officials insist that the animals should be forcibly removed by a 'horse haulier at the appointed time'.

This curious episode is the latest move in a protracted legal dispute between Miss Williams and the council over the ownership of the field. Miss Williams claims that she bought the field, Sweatford Water, from a local farmer, Chubby Butler, in November 1963 in return for £500 and twenty steers, and has used it ever since to keep her horses. The contract, written in pencil, reads 'Payed by Miss F.W. Williams £500 and 20 beef calves for Sweatford field about 5 acres, W.C. Butler'. But, long after Butler's death, the deeds of the farm, of which the field had been part, passed after a company bankruptcy to the Treasury Solicitor who, in 1991, sold the field to the New Forest District Council for £100 (earlier the council had approached Miss Williams with an offer to buy the field from her for housing development). In May 1993, a district court judge, Mr Justice Griffiths, heard an action in which Miss Williams represented herself, and found in favour of the council's claim that it had title to the field, on the grounds that the pencilled document did not constitute a valid contract. According to Miss Williams, on 15 June she instructed her solicitors to lodge an appeal, but they did not do so. Only in August did she manage to recover her papers to instruct a new solicitor, who suggested that she should seek leave to appeal 'out of time' on the grounds that, because she was not versed in the law, her case had not been properly heard.

Meanwhile, officials of the New Forest Council are proceeding to take possession of the field on the appointed day. After angry exchanges, in which Miss Hennell suffers severe bruising when the field gate is pushed against her, the council representatives manage to push the horses in the box, to boos from onlookers. After the short journey, the 25-year-old Comanche, which had to be sedated by a vet before it would enter the box, is in a 'very poor way', and 'stands with her head on the ground, covered in foam'. The following day the vet discovers that the pony's jaw is broken, and she haemorrhages for several hours while the vet battles to save her life. A New Forest environmental health technician, Mr Weldyoz, who has been present at the eviction, says that the council now plans to 'develop the land into a park for the Fordingbridge area'.

Following this episode, Miss Williams was informed that she now owed the New Forest District Council £38,000 for its legal costs in fighting the case.

*　　*　　*

In Southampton in February 1993, Dr Miller, the managing director of Cymbus Bioscience Ltd, is talking to a visiting professor from the University of Wales when two men enter his office without an appointment. One of them, Mr Nash, explains that they are officials of the Inland Revenue and have come to collect the arrears owed by the firm on PAYE and National Insurance. This is said in front of the professor and members of staff. Dr Miller explains that the company does not owe any money to the Inland Revenue, and suggests that Mr Nash goes back to his office to confirm his facts. Mr Nash persists in claiming that the firm owes the money he has the authority to collect, until Dr Miller puts through a call to the local tax office to speak to his usual inspector, Mrs Doherty, with whom the firm has always had good relations. Mrs Doherty is happy to confirm over the telephone to Mr Nash that Cymbus Bioscience is fully paid up and that all is in order. The two officials then leave Dr Miller's office, without apology or any expression of regret for their intrusion.

*　　*　　*

For more than 150 years the Atrill family, boatbuilders of Bembridge, Isle of White, have been running a tiny ferry service across the harbour to St Helen's. At 35p a passenger, the service makes no profit but is much appreciated by locals and holiday-makers. It has been operated for many years by Gordon Atrill, who served in minesweepers on the Arctic convoys during the Second World War.

One day in August 1993, when it is pouring with rain, a man arrives introducing himself as a Mr Murphy, the 'Licensing Officer' of Medina District Council. He presents Mr Atrill with some papers and switches on a tape recorder, informing him that he will have to pay an annual licence fee of £40, plus £20 for a 'safety inspection', and a further £15 for a licence plate. He is also required to submit a plan of the vessel showing the whereabouts of all safety equipment. Two days later, these demands are confirmed by a letter which refers throughout to Bembridge harbour as 'Cambridge harbour'. Mr Atrill recalls that, under the nineteenth century Bembridge Harbour Act, the ferry service was permitted to operate 'free of all charges'. But this appears to carry no weight with the official, who informs Mr Atrill that if he is caught carrying passengers without a licence he will be liable for a fine of up to £400 for each trip made 'illegally'. Mr Atrill reluctantly concludes that he cannot afford the expense and time involved in complying with Mr Murphy's demands, or in fighting them. At the end of August 1993, the service operated by his great-great-grandfather (and possibly by generations before that) comes to an end.

*   *   *

This is our first example of the innumerable successful businesses closed down by the EHOs as they launched their 1992 'hygiene blitz'. No one – certainly not the government – bothered to keep a record of how many businesses and other food-handling operations were closed down at the time, for no benefit in food safety, but it must have run into thousands.

In Basingstoke in August 1992, the oldest established pork butcher in England, Griffins, finally closes its doors. The shop has been doing very good business but, like countless other butchers, bakers, fishmongers and other food shops all over Britain, it has been instructed by EHOs under the Food Safety Act 1990 to carry out 'improvements' for hygiene purposes. These would cost more than the shop could afford. Mrs June Vines, the owner of Griffins, has been told that to stay in business she will have to strip away all the traditional patterned tiles from the shop's interior, and replace all floors, walls and ceiling with 'seamless cladding'. She will either have to install very expensive new cooling systems, or keep all her meat sealed and tucked away in a refrigerated cold room, out of customers' sight. 'We are being asked to turn our butcher's shop into an operating theatre', says Mrs Vines, as she puts up the shutters for the last time on the Georgian building which has housed the business since 1756.

*　　*　　*

Here was another disaster involving thousands of small businesses. Again the claimed justification was 'safety'.

In Selsey, the Treasure Chest, a second-hand furniture business run by John Connor, did so well in 1992 that, at the beginning of 1993, he signs a lease on a second shop. He is then notified by local trading standards officers that, under the DTI's new Furniture and Furnishings (Fire) (Safety) (Amendment) Regulations 1992, it will no longer be legal for him to see almost any upholstered furniture made between 1950 and 1988, because it does not meet the latest fire safety standards. This means that hundreds of thousands of items of second-hand furniture sold each year in shops, auctions and car-boot sales will now have to be burned, or buried in landfill sites. Since most of Mr Connor's trade is in such items, he has to close his business down. Amongst many other traders similarly hit are charity shops, such as the seventeen furniture shops run by Oxfam, raising £400,000 a year, which have to close.

What made this regulation particularly absurd was that most of the furniture made between 1950 and 1988 was still quite legally being used in private homes. It was only covered by the new law when offered for sale (but see also the entry under 'Llandysal, Dyfed').

*   *   *

In 1993, the 500 members of the Bognor Golf Club in Sussex are still reeling from the after-effects of a crisis brought on the club two years earlier, when they had wished to make some improvements to the bar and restaurant of their club house. Before plans were drawn up it had been suggested that it might be sensible to ask for advice from the environmental health department of the local Arun District Council. An EHO came to look round and a few weeks later, to their astonishment, each of the club's committee members and office holders received a bulging envelope containing 108 pages. The council had sent out in all some 2000 pieces of paper. These comprised copies of thirty-six 'Improvement Notices', twenty-two under the Food Safety Act 1990 and fourteen under the Health and Safety at Work Act 1974, giving the club just two months to carry out a long list of works or be closed down. It seemed highly questionable what most of the requirements had to do with hygiene or safety. But it appeared that the official had the power to require the works, and not to comply with a statutory Improvement Notice under these circumstances would have been a criminal

offence, punishable by fines or imprisonment. The works ended up costing the club's members well over £100,000.

*   *   *

This is the first example of the devastating impact of the Children Act 1989 on Britain's privately run nursery schools. While the social workers ran riot, state-run schools remained unaffected.

In the village of Coombes, West Sussex, the Old Rectory Nursery School has been run for sixteen years by Brianne Reeve, a Froebel-trained teacher with thirty years experience. In the summer and autumn of 1992, she is visited by county council social workers who have come to enforce new Department of Health guidelines under the Children Act 1989, designed to give additional protection to children after the Cleveland affair and the other 'child abuse' cases of the 1980s. Mrs Reeve is told to carry out a long list of 'safety' requirements. These include placing a 'cover' over a small pond in her garden where she teaches children about wildlife, and spending more than £1000 on what she considers to be unnecessary fencing and 'stair-gates'. She is ordered to send one of her assistants on a course costing £50 which includes learning how to use 'playdough', and told that any man who might come into contact with her children must be first checked by the police. This includes her husband, a local headmaster, and her 91-year-old father-in-law. Because Mrs Reeve cannot reach agreement on the demands, the social workers will not register the school, as is now required under the Act. She is therefore no longer allowed to admit new children. Although she has hitherto had a long waiting list because her school is so popular, by January 1993 she is down to five pupils. The social workers have now informed her that her Grade II listed house will 'probably not pass the fire regulations for registration next year'.

*   *   *

Another example of a bizarre EEC scheme which Britain's officials managed to implement in a far more cumbersome and costly fashion than anywhere else in Europe.

In a greenhouse in West Sussex owned by Madestein UK, a plant nursery firm, the managing director Peter Zwinkels in July 1993 watches an official of MAFF's Plant Health and Seeds Inspectorate examining 200,000 tiny cabbage plants. When he has completed his task, for which the company has to pay £70 an hour, the official returns to Mr Zwinkels' office to give the plants their new 'plant passports', allowing the firm to sell this batch anywhere in the UK or other EEC countries. As from 1 July 1993, under the Plants Health Regulations, implementing EEC Directive 77/93 (with its twenty-five subsequent amendments), professional plant growers in Britain are only permitted to trade in plants when they have a passport recording each batch of plants, where in the nursery the plants were grown and many other details. (At least this is an improvement on the original proposals, when it looked as if every single plant sold would have to be separately documented.) The purpose of the directive is to give official control over plants which might carry disease. But, as UK growers point out, no other country in Europe has set up such cumbersome arrangements for implementing the EEC law. If growers in Spain or Italy wish to export plants to Britain, they can provide their own documentation. And under the new Single Market rules, there is no longer any control to stop them sending to Britain anything they wish.

*   *   *

Arguably no group in Britain faced a more nightmarish future as a result of our membership of the EEC than our fishermen. By the same general principle that 'hygiene' measures did nothing for hygiene, 'safety' measures did nothing for safety, and 'environmental protection' measures did nothing for the environment, so did measures to 'conserve fish stocks' ensure that fish stocks would be plundered more recklessly than ever.

On a Sunday morning in May 1993, drivers along the Hastings seafront are startled to see a ten-ton fishing boat high and dry on the promenade. It is festooned with effigies and slogans distinctly unflattering to local Tory MP Jacqui Lait and the fisheries ministers John Gummer and David Curry. *The Golden Sovereign* has been hauled onto the land by local fishermen to register the fact that thousands of fishermen all over Britain have just been told by MAFF that in future they will only be allowed to earn their living for eighty days in a year. As they immediately recognize, this means most will be forced to give up fishing altogether. Because everyone is similarly affected, they will not be able to sell their boats. They will be left without assets or livelihood, owing large sums to the bank or on mortgages which they cannot hope to repay. The fishermen have been forced into this extraordinary situation by powers to limit their 'days at sea' taken by the Government under the Sea Fish Conservation Act 1992, put through by Mr Gummer and Mr Curry and supported by almost all Conservative MPs, including Miss Lait. The supposed justification for this Act is an agreement reached in Brussels in December 1992 that all EEC countries should reduce their 'fishing effort' to conserve fish stocks in EEC waters.

But what enrages the Hastings fishermen – and thousands of others similarly affected in all parts of Britain – is not only the knowledge that eighty per cent of those stocks are in waters which until 1972 were solely British. They cannot understand, firstly, why Britain has now agreed to reduce its 'fishing effort' by a larger percentage – nineteen per cent – than any other EEC country (Spain, with a fleet eight times larger than Britain's, only has to cut back by four per cent). Secondly, they see that other countries are achieving their reduction by drawing on huge sums of EEC money to compensate fishermen who agree to give up fishing. Only Britain has adopted the extraordinary tactic of simply forbidding fishermen to work for up to nine months of the year, knowing that this will drive thousands of them out of business without the government having to pay compensation (in fact the UK Government has also introduced a modest compensation scheme but this is nothing like enough to achieve the overall reduction to which Gummer and Curry have agreed).

But what finally drives the British fishermen to despair is their knowledge that the closing down of a large part of the British fishing fleet will do nothing to conserve fish stocks whatsoever. The net result of the policy adopted by Gummer and Curry will simply be that, as British fishermen are forced into bankruptcy, their licences and fishing quotas will be bought up by Dutch, French and Spanish companies, operating under much less rigorous conservation control (in Britain there are nearly 200 fisheries inspectors to ensure that no fisherman catches more than his quote; in Spain there are only seventeen, all said to be based in Madrid). In a few years time, it seems likely that the only fishing boats off Hastings and much of the coast of Britain will be those belonging to our EEC 'partners'.

*   *   *

One of the most under-reported stories of 1992 and 1993 was the threat hanging over thousands of successful British companies from the absurdly exacting standards for 'air pollution' laid down by Brussels, and faithfully implemented by the D.o.E under the Environmental Protection Act. While most of Britain's major sources of pollution, such as twenty million road vehicles, remained unaffected, many small companies faced the prospect of closure. Here is an example.

In St Leonards, Surrey Roll Leaf Ltd makes foil films used for printing on a wide range of products from cartons to book covers. Founded in 1976 by its managing director Graham Hirst, the company turns over £1.5 million and sells successfully, against tough international competition, to customers all over the world. In September 1992, SRL's manufacturing process catches the eye of Mr Hawes, an EHO from Hastings Borough Council. Because the process gives off tiny amounts of non-toxic chemicals to the air, classified under the Environmental Protection Act 1990 as volatile organic compounds, or VOCs, this means, as Mr Hawes informs the company, that it must now be 'authorized' by the local authority in order to stay in business. This requires payment of a £900 fee with an annual 'subsistence fee' of £550. The level of VOCs – mainly alcohol – given off by SRL's process is so low that it only equates to a tenth of that emitted from a car engine. But Mr Hawes says that SRL must cut its emissions to a level equivalent to 150th of a car engine emission by 1997. Thus, SRL will be required to produce less alcohol from their process than is permitted in the breath of a car driver. If they do not do this, they will be closed down. To achieve the level required, SRL discovers that it will have to install cumbersome 'afterburners', at a cost of £700,000, to incinerate the VOCs before they reach the outside air. But so diluted are the VOCs given off that they will have to be concentrated before they can be burnt effectively. Incineration would also burn large quantities of gas, which would produce more pollution than the process would save. It makes no sense in environmental terms and would be so expensive that the company would have to close down, putting thirty-three people out of work. Mr Hawes replies that this is not his concern. His duty is to enforce the regulations.

*　　*　　*

In Dover, Harbour Board staff are puzzling over how they can comply with new MAFF regulations governing the dumping at sea of spoil from dredging operations. This can only be done under licence, the cost of which is soaring. In 1985, a three-year licence cost only £165. Since 1989, the MAFF licence has been for one year only, and now costs £2800. But what particularly baffles them is a new requirement that all spoil dumping must be electronically logged with a Marine Position Recorder, or MPR. The problem is that such a device is simply not available. The electronics firm Ferranti was asked to design one but had discovered that, to meet the MAFF specifications, it would be too expensive to produce. This had not deterred MAFF officials from introducing a legal requirement to use an instrument that is not yet in existence.

*　　*　　*

Also in Dover, as the great day of the European Single Market arrives on 1 January 1993, local health officers are told that they no longer have to inspect all foodstuffs coming into the port, to check whether they are fit to eat. In 1992, EHOs in British ports found 22,000 tonnes of food imported from EEC countries that was unfit. But now, under Single Market rules, it is illegal for British port authorities to carry out routine checks on food at points of entry from the EEC. This means, according to Professor Verner Wheelock, Director of the Food Policy Unit at Bradford University, that large quantities of unsafe food may now be freely imported, some of which may not be discovered until people all over Britain suffer from food-poisoning.

*   *   *

As another consequence of the Single Market, HM Customs and Excise officials no longer keep records of goods leaving and entering Britain in the course of trade with other EEC countries. But the records still have to be kept and the responsibility now falls on firms trading with the EEC themselves. Under a new system known as 'Intrastats', firms trading goods or services must supply a quarterly return known as an 'Aggregated Sales Listing', showing values of all exports, listing the customers to whom they are sent with their VAT numbers (this even applies, for instance, to subscribers to newspapers like the *Wall Street Journal*, who could run into tens of thousands). In addition, every month, firms must complete a 'Supplementary Statistical Declaration'. This must show the exact nature, quantity and value of all exports and imports, plus many other details, requiring reference for guidance to a 750-page book produced by Customs and Excise. Severe penalties can be imposed for any forms returned more than two weeks late. Customs and Excise estimate that the cost of this to British firms will be not more than £100 million a year. But one leading firm of London accountants, Coopers and Lybrand, estimate that the additional costs to their clients alone – many of whom are having to take on additional staff to cope with the paperwork – will be £30–40 million. More reliable estimates of the total cost to British firms are 'over £1 billion'.

*   *   *

Arguably, the purest distillation of bureaucracy for its own sake in Britain in 1992 and 1993 was the system known as BS 5750. No one could provide a convincing explanation as

*to what purpose it served. It was immensely damaging. Yet
every week, more and more firms got sucked into it, like some
mad chain letter to which few dared say no.*

From his home in Strood, Tim Leeder runs a business as a
plumbing and heating engineer, with his wife Linda providing
secretarial backup. In November 1992, he receives a letter
from his trade association advising him that, within a year
or two, it may be difficult for businesses like his to survive
unless they have a certificate stating that their 'management
methods and production systems' meet the 'quality standard'
of something called BS 5750. As a first step, Mr Leeder can
go on a course in the north of England which will cost him
£1250 and take up a day a month for a year. Then he will
have to draw up a written manual, explaining all his 'systems'
and 'the pattern of responsibility' in his company. Then he
will have to pay anything between £700 and £1500 to a
'certificating body' for his certificate. All this sounds like the
purest gobbledygook to the man running a two-person
plumbing business from his home and a shed in the back
garden. What is this, in section 4.1.2.2 – 'The supplier shall
identify in-house verification requirements, providing
adequate resources and assigned trained personnel for verification activities'? Presumably, this will be Linda's job – she
is 'in-house', while Tim is 'in-shed'. But the more Mr Leeder
hears about BS 5750, the more alarmed he becomes – particularly by the threat that, before long, it may be impossible to
carry on in business without this mysterious accreditation,
because companies which have it will only be prepared to do
business with others which have joined the same freemasonry.
Certainly the BS 5750 craze – actively and financially encouraged by the officials of the DTI – seems to be spreading, like
some Japanese knotweed, through businesses and organizations of all shapes and sizes. It is expensive, time-consuming,

generates an enormous amount of paperwork. One company in Birmingham is said to have no fewer than fifteen of its forty employees working full-time on BS 5750. Yet, as everyone agrees, the most extraordinary thing is that having a BS 5750 certificate does not guarantee in any way the quality of goods or services a business provides to its customers. It merely shows that the company is complying with the paperwork and procedures which it itself has drawn up for its own operations – usually in conjunction with highly expensive management consultants. It seems that companies are prepared to half-strangle themselves in the entrails of this incomprehensible monster, for no purpose whatsoever except to avoid losing business from other companies engaged in the same act of suicide.

*   *   *

This is a perfect example of how Whitehall officials zealously implemented EEC directives without a thought for the damage they might do to small British firms.

Near Rochester, Kent, Colman Twohig, who runs a business designing and supplying one-off electronic devices for use in dredging and hydrographic surveying, is looking at new regulations issued by the DTI, to implement EEC Directive 89/336, on 'electromagnetic compatibility'. The directive's purpose, of which Mr Twohig approves, is to ensure that no piece of electrical equipment gives off signals which might interfere with others. But when, in November 1992, Mr Twohig examines guidance notes on how the DTI is proposing to implement this directive, he becomes increasingly alarmed. It seems he will have to send off each separate item of equipment he assembles, often costing as little as £50 or less, to an 'approved testing house', which will cost him up to £1000 a day. If this guidance means what it appears to mean, there is no way he or thousands of other similar small specialized electronics firms can afford to stay in business. Furthermore, it seems that only one other country in the EEC, Germany, even has serious plans to implement the directive at all. When Mr Twohig rings up the DTI, the relevant official, Mr McCosh, eventually agrees that Mr Twohig may well be right. It does look as though the effect of the new regulations will be to put him and others out of business. But Mr McCosh tries to console Twohig with the assurance that this had not been the DTI's intention when it was considering how the directive should be carried out.

Following coverage of their plight in the Sunday Telegraph, *the DTI announced in January 1993 that it was changing its 'guidance' to allow small firms to carry out their own testing.*

*   *   *

We are familiar with examples of how Whitehall officials were so eager to comply with EEC directives that they would go further than Brussels in drawing up UK regulations. Here was a variation on the theme – where UK officials repeatedly flouted EEC law and Brussels directives, in order to continue penalizing hundreds of small charitable bodies in Britain which they must have calculated would not have the practical means to challenge them in the European Court of Justice.

In Orpington, Ernest Virgo, a retired MAFF civil servant, is secretary of the Kent Playing Fields Association, a voluntary society representing non profit-making local sports clubs. Like thousands of similar clubs all over Britain, these have to pay VAT on their operations which, when they are building a new pavilion or installing hard tennis courts, can amount to thousands of pounds. Mr Virgo has discovered that when VAT was introduced in 1973, as part of Britain's joining the

EEC, it was Brussels' view that non profit-making bodies like the sports clubs should be exempted, a ruling with which all the other Member States have complied. But on the insistence of HM Customs and Excise, Britain was given a temporary 'derogation', allowing the sports clubs to be charged. When this 'derogation' lapsed, Customs and Excise went on charging the clubs VAT, to the point where the EEC's eighteenth VAT Directive had to make it specifically clear that, as from 1 January 1990, Britain had no legal right under EEC law to do so. Although in 1989 the Court of Appeal confirmed that, under British law, a non profit-making organization is defined in exactly the same way as it is under EEC law, the officials of Customs and Excise refused to accept the Brussels ruling. No doubt they hoped the small sports clubs would be reluctant to pay out the large sums in legal fees necessary to mount a challenge in the courts. In November 1992, Mr Virgo claims that Treasury ministers have been repeatedly misinformed about what is going on, that the British government has been guilty of 'serious maladministration' and that the money charged by Customs and Excise since 1990 should be refunded. In July 1993, as a result of his campaign, a junior Treasury minister, Sir John Cope, finally agrees that the matter should be looked at again. But there is no mention of compensation for the millions of pounds the VAT men have raised illegally since 1990.

* * *

In Hampstead, Elizabeth Gundrey has for twelve years been compiling *Staying Off The Beaten Track*, a well-known guide to high-quality bed and breakfast houses and small private hotels all over Britain. Most of these establishments, ranging from manor houses to farmhouses, are like private homes which take in guests – but in 1992 their proprietors have been reporting a deluge of new problems with officialdom in all directions. High on the list has been the 'hygiene blitz' waged by EHOs. As one proprietor writes from Norfolk, 'Breckland District Council are driving us mad with their petty interpretation of new hygiene regulations'. The EHOs have been prohibiting cookery books in kitchens, banning wooden shelves, chopping boards and spoons, and ordering the covering up of flagstone floors with vinyl. Small guest houses are being told that it is acceptable to cook breakfasts in the family kitchen but if dinner is served a new, separate kitchen will have to be installed. One lady in Earl Soham, Suffolk, has a kitchen so small that, when she was ordered to install a second sink, the works would have required knocking down the external wall of the house. Because in the previous year she only had two guests, she decided to abandon bed and breakfasts. Other worries range from the charging of business rates on guest houses with only three bedrooms to the exorbitant demands of fire officers. But the most widespread complaint of all is the system whereby proprietors must pay £75 to be inspected by local tourist boards, in order to qualify for lists of 'recommended accommodation'. Although the inspectors are meant only to check off available facilities to see how many 'crowns' each establishment rates, a near universal complaint is how the inspectors go beyond their brief, demanding anything from 'written breakfast menus' to 'matching sets of furniture and upholstery'. In Co. Durham, one inspector criticizes Victorian four-poster beds for having 'old fashioned frames'. In Suffolk a lady in her 70s is told to turn her single rooms into doubles and doubles into singles. In Norfolk, an inspector condemns a handsome Georgian manor house for being 'very severe' and suggests putting in new windows 'with curved features' – on a listed building. From all over Britain, Mrs Gundry's proprietors are writing to say that they are dropping out of the tourist board system, because too many inspectors are 'unsympathetic',

'arrogant', 'a pain in the neck' and because 'for all the custom we get as a result, it is not worth the trouble'.

*   *   *

Yet another example of how the coming of the Single Market, hailed as a move towards 'liberalizing trade', only meant for many a huge increase in paperwork, without any gain whatsoever.

In Islington, north London, the international opera singer David Wilson-Johnson is informed by his local VAT office in February 1993 of another consequence of the Single Market. It will now be necessary for him to register individually for VAT in all of the twelve EEC Member States, instead of only in the UK as previously. This means that he will have to send in regular returns to the VAT authorities in each of the twelve countries, even if he had not earned any money in that country in the period in question – with a penalty for any days that his returns are late. There seems to be considerable confusion as to what rate the services of an opera singer should be charged at – as in Italy, where VAT percentage rates are 0, 4, 9, 12, 19 or 38. He writes off dutifully to all the national VAT authorities, and two months later has had only two replies. One from Holland begins, in English, 'If you are a natural, what is your date of birth?' The other is in such dense bureaucratic German that, even though Mr Wilson-Johnson is a linguist, he has to send it off for translation.

*   *   *

MAFF's notorious efforts to over-implement the EEC's meat hygiene directive may have spread havoc through the meat industry all over Britain – but it was unlikely to claim any victims more celebrated than this one.

In Smithfield, the owners of the famous meat market, the City of London Corporation, have spent £25 million on the first stage of a £60 million scheme to bring the market into line with the new structural requirements under MAFF's Fresh Meat (Hygiene and Inspection) Regulations 1992. To pay for the 'improvements', tenants of the East Market will each have to pay £215,000 in the first year, a 600 per cent increase on their previous rental payments. When the deadline for their decision arrives on 16 April 1993, none have been able to afford the vast rise in costs. The City faces the prospect of opening its refurbished building in April 1994 with no tenants.

*   *   *

In Thayer Street, Marylebone, in the summer of 1993, many shops stand empty. The area has been badly hit both by the recession and by an explosion of local crime and vandalism, which the police seem powerless to halt. But in July 1993, there is evidence that at least someone is determined to enforce the law. Mr Butterfield, head of Westminster City Council's Consumer Protection Division, has sent out a small army of twenty-two 'enforcement officers' to check that traders are complying with the Price Marking Regulations 1991, implementing EEC Directive 88/314. Picking her way past twenty-six empty shops, one of these officials, Ms Liane Mernane, comes across one of the few surviving businesses in Thayer Street, a high-class dress shop owned by Helen Thomas, who is particularly admired for the artistry of her window displays. Ms Mernane enters the shop and points out that the price tickets on the goods in the window are illegal because they are not clearly visible. Mrs Thomas explains that she does not wish to put the tickets on the front of the dresses and jackets, partly for aesthetic reasons and partly because she does not want to tempt thieves, who have already broken into her shop three times.

Two days later, Mrs Thomas receives a letter from Mr Butterfield pointing out that she is in breach of the law, and may face criminal prosecution. Her immediate response is to clear the window, and put up a large sign reading 'Lack of window display by order of Westminster Council and EEC'. A day or two later she is just about to restock the window, ostentatiously pricing her goods in ecus, when the lawyer upstairs shows her a judgement reported in that morning's *Times*. Following an appeal against conviction in a similar case, Lord Justice Watkins has ruled that, so long as price markings are available, they do not have to be visible. If a customer can be shown them by an assistant, this is within the law. It seems that Mrs Thomas has been saved from criminal prosecution in the nick of time.

Shortly afterwards, Mrs Thomas received from the DTI a 'consultation document' on proposed amendments to the Price Marking Regulations. One of these sought to emphasize that it definitely should be a criminal offence for price tickets to be available only in such a way that a customer has to ask to see them. The learned judge, it seemed, had ruled in vain.

*   *   *

Off the Strand in November 1992, Edward Baldwin of A.H. Baldwin, one of London's leading coin dealers, is describing as 'completely mad' a proposed EEC directive covering the exporting of old coins. Under the Brussels proposals, dealers will have to obtain a separate export licence for each old coin they export, regardless of value. 'If these rules go through', says Mr Baldwin, 'and I want to sell 500 common Roman coins worth £1 each to an American dealer, I will have to supply a separate licence for every single one of them'. The trade estimates that the Department of National Heritage will have to issue 250,000 licences a year. Only after the coin dealers have spent nightmarish months wondering how they can cope with the paperwork, and lobbying officials as to the disaster this directive will bring on their trade, does common sense for once prevail. At a Council of Ministers meeting on 10 November, the officials are overruled and the requirement for each coin to have its own passport is dropped.

*   *   *

In Chelsea, the head of the local CID, Chief Inspector Colin Ritchie, is trying to explain in March 1993 how the police are finding it increasingly difficult to concentrate on fighting rising crime because they are swamped in an ever-rising sea of bureaucracy. Once an officer takes on a new case, the paperwork required is now so great that it is unlikely that he or she will be able to do anything else that day. Inspector Ritchie shows how, in order to bring the prosecution of one simple case of assault, it has been necessary to fill in '135 different forms'. When found guilty, the accused man was fined £1.60.

*   *   *

In Putney, Trufree Foods, who make special dietary flours, have received a letter from Wandsworth Borough Council trading standards department confirming that trading standards officials in another local authority have raised an 'objection' to their packaging. This carries a panel stating that the net weight of the flour in their packets is '1Kg'. It is pointed out that 'the weight should be expressed in the lower case form of "1kg" instead of the capital, "1Kg"'. The total cost of 'putting this dreadful crime to rights', as the company

puts it, will be £6000, involving seven different packs, new typesetting, film, plates and the destruction of existing packs. 'Fortunately', they go on, 'in Wandsworth we are blessed with a TSO who has common sense – a rare animal indeed'. As a special concession, the company is permitted to continue using the offending packs until existing supplies are exhausted.

*　　*　　*

One morning in May 1993, the residents of Challoner Crescent, Fulham, are concerned to see that someone has fly-tipped a large pile of rubbish on the corner of their street. As dutiful citizens, they report this to their local council, Hammersmith and Fulham. Meanwhile, they collect up the rubbish in plastic sacks for the dustmen to remove on their usual collection day, Tuesday. Shortly afterwards, twenty residents are startled to receive summonses through the post on criminal charges of illegally dumping rubbish under the Control of Pollution Act 1974. Their offence, it seems, lies in the fact that they had left out the rubbish on Tuesday 4 May whereas, thanks to a bank holiday, that day's collection had been put back to Wednesday 5 May. By an Alice in Wonderland twist, the council officials state that, by leaving out the rubbish on a Tuesday, the residents had broken a council regulation laying down that rubbish may only legally be put out for collection 'on a Tuesday'. Three months later, the residents all appear at Walton Street Magistrates' Court. They hear the prosecuting counsel claim that they were all guilty of criminal behaviour because they 'should have realized that, because of the bank holiday, the collection day was Wednesday'. The magistrates dismiss the charges, at a cost to chargepayers of several thousand pounds.

*　　*　　*

Thousands of British firms found in 1992 that they were becoming increasingly enmeshed in cumbersome and costly paperwork to obtain 'British Standards' and other certificates which were now necessary before they could sell their products. A frequent complaint was having to pay for officials to fly all over the world to check on components used. Another was the lack of professional competence shown by certifying bodies. Here is a typical example.

In Amersham, Bucks, a small engineering company, Yorkpark Ltd, has produced three successful new designs for hot water cylinders, which it is selling at home and abroad. The firm has had to pay £25,000 to a body called the British Board of Agrement to obtain certificates showing that the cylinders comply with British building regulations. This included paying for officials to fly to Germany and Austria. Now, in December 1992, Yorkpark is told that, although the designs have not changed, it must pay a further £4000 to the BBA so that the certificates can be 'reviewed'. When managing director Ian Rodger enquires why the extra work is necessary, on top of the 'horrifically expensive' cost of the original certificates, he is told by BBA officials that they are having to 'rewrite the certificates with new drawings' and carry out a 'consumer survey', at Yorkpark's expense. Yorkpark is told that unless it agrees to the additional payment within three weeks, the certificates already issued will be withdrawn.

While this is still under discussion, in January 1993, an EHO arrives unannounced in Mr Rodger's office and asks to see the inventory of 'hazardous substances' which the company is obliged to keep under the Control of Substances Hazardous to Health Regulations 1988, known as COSHH. These were introduced by the Health and Safety Executive to implement EEC Directive 80/1107, designed to protect workers from 'risks related to exposure to chemical, physical and biological agents'. Yorkpark's inventory appears to be deficient. 'What', the EHO asks Mr Rodger, 'do you use for washing up?' 'Fairy Liquid', Rodger replies. 'That should go down on your list', the EHO solemnly advises. It is suggested that 80/1107 should be known in future as 'the Fairy Liquid Directive'.

* * *

In Richmond-upon-Thames, Thomas Hunter-Weir is a wine merchant, specializing in New Zealand wines. In March 1993, he is visited by a council official to ask how he disposes of his 'industrial waste'. Mr Hunter-Weir says he has no 'industrial waste', only the cardboard boxes in which his wine is delivered. Once a month he folds these flat and takes them off to the council recycling centre. The official points out that, as from 1 April, under the new Environmental Protection Act, this will be a criminal offence, liable to an unlimited fine. Any 'waste' produced by a business paying the business rate can only be removed by someone holding a Waste Carrier's License. A 'Controlled Waste Transfer Note' must be completed and signed by both parties for each transaction, stating the exact nature, quantity and weight of the waste, where the transfer takes place and the full name and addresses of both parties – and these documents have to be kept, available for inspection at any time, for a period of two years. Mr Hunter-Weir is puzzled as to how this procedure, generating an ever-growing mass of paper, will give greater protection to the 'environment' than his monthly visits to the recycling centre.

* * *

On 1 January 1993, to celebrate the arrival of the Single Market, the Health and Safety Executive introduced no fewer than six new sets of regulations, to implement a stack of health and safety directives. The HSE's own estimate of what

*it would cost British industry to comply with these was a
mere £540 million in the first year. Many experts begged to
differ, talking of 'many billions' – except that many of the
provisions were so far-fetched that it was highly unlikely that
any British firms would comply in full. Here is an estimate
of what it would cost one organization to meet all the requirements of just one of these new sets of regulations.*

At the University of Surrey, in the autumn of 1992, an assistant principal in the university administration, Mr Brian Barnard, is looking at the Health and Safety (Display Screen
Equipment) Regulations 1992, implementing EEC Directive
90/270. These relate to the 'health and safety' of employees
using VDU screens, stipulating that 'workstations' must comply with certain standards of space, lighting, noise and design,
including approved designs for desks and chairs. A full 'health
and safety analysis' must be carried out for each employee
and workstation, with records kept. Employees must be given
a ten-minute break from their screens each hour and can
request an eye test and spectacles, to be paid for by their
employers. Mr Barnard does a rough calculation of what it
would cost the University of Surrey to comply with these new
regulations. He arrives at a figure of £900,000.

* * *

*Here was another hidden disaster from the EEC's moves to
'harmonise' trade in the new Single Market, as relentlessly
implemented by UK officials.*

In Weybridge, Dr Wasses Mansi, a 73-year-old former
research officer at the Ministry of Agriculture, is the only
producer in Britain of a vaccine against myxomatosis, which
he makes in a laboratory in his garden. Over the past thirty-
three years, his Weyvak has saved the lives of thousands of

pet rabbits from the killer disease, but in April 1992 Dr Mansi is forced to stop production because he can no longer afford to comply with ever-increasing requirements imposed on him by MAFF's Veterinary Medicines Directorate. Some months later, as rabbit breeders and vets all over Britain discover that supplies of Weyvak are exhausted and that no myxomatosis vaccine is now available, Dr Mansi apologizes to pet-owners but explains that in recent years he had been 'visited by a new breed of officials armed with computers and using jargon I could not understand'. They had told him that if he wished to keep his licence he would have to modernize his equipment, improve his buildings and keep much more detailed paper-work, 'which would have involved me getting staff'. What particularly puzzled Dr Mansi is that in early years the Ministry of Agriculture had given him nothing but encouragement for providing such a valuable service and there has never been any complaint about his product. Yet now MAFF seems quite unconcerned that Britain's rabbit owners are being left without any protection against the disease. And they are by no means the only animal owners who are suddenly finding their animals deprived of veterinary treatments which have proved their worth over the years. Under an EEC directive on the harmonization of licensing, MAFF's Veterinary Medicines Directorate has called in for review 2727 products which first obtained licences before 1984. Because companies cannot afford to pay up to £100,000 for the voluminous documentation involved in applying for renewals, the licences for 1720 products have already been abandoned and only 727 have been renewed. Yet under the same directive, other governments have been renewing licences almost automatically.

* * *

Another relatively small industry hard-hit by Britain's membership of the EEC was beekeeping. Beekeepers faced a

*whole range of problems, from subsidies given to their conti-
nental competitors to help fight the deadly varroa mite, to
having to pay £700 a tonne for sugar in the highly protected
EEC market, when their competitors outside the EEC only
had to pay the £150 a tonne world price. But one well-known
bee expert had a more particular problem with the officials
of MAFF.*

At Burghfield, Berkshire, Oliver Field, one of Britain's best-
known beekeepers, is engaged in a battle in June 1993 to stop
MAFF officials coming onto his honey farm to test his 500
hives for signs of 'foul brood', a bacterial disease which can
devastate bee colonies. The reason why Mr Field is so adam-
ant that the officials should not enter his farm is that when
they came in March 1992 they dosed six of his hives with
the antibacterial syrups used to cure 'foul brood', at four
times the required strength. This resulted in more than a quarter of a million of his bees dying, and the loss of £3000-worth
of honey production. The proper way to keep the disease in
check, says Mr Field, a noted authority on beekeeping who has
published books on bees and supplies Sainsburys with honey,
is to treat the bees regularly to prevent the bacteria getting a
hold. 'I used to do that successfully myself', Mr Field explains,
'but now under the ministry's Bee Control Order, it is illegal
for me to do so'. The Order also gives ministry officials the right
to enter farms to check the hives at any time. But after Mr
Field's experience in 1992, for which the ministry has never
apologized nor offered any explanation, he is now prepared to
face prosecution and even a prison sentence rather than risk
any repetition of their blunder.

*   *   *

In Wokingham, in March 1993, Miss Tucker, a pensioner,
goes into the local Waitrose supermarket and asks for a single

slice of ham, as she has often done before. She is astonished to be told that she will have to buy a second slice, because the weight of the first is under 1¼ oz., and under new 'EEC regulations' it is no longer legal to sell anything weighing less than 1¼ oz.. She cannot believe what she is hearing, but it is true. Like other supermarkets, Waitrose has been instructed that it must now comply with the DTI's Weighing Machines (Non-Automatic Weighing Machines) Regulations 1988, brought in to implement EEC Directive 90/384 on the 'harmonisation of laws relating to non-automatic weighing instruments'. The officials have decreed that because it is difficult to measure small weights with scientifically precise accuracy it is much better to protect 'consumers' by forbidding them to buy goods in such small quantities at all – even if, like Miss Tucker, that is what they want.

*   *   *

Again, the EHOs are pursuing their obsession with 'unhygienic' wood.

At Dorney, Buckinghamshire, Leslie and Barbara Ainsworth have for many years run the Danette's boarding kennels for dogs. They have recently spent nearly £8000 to keep their thirty-one wooden kennels in top condition. But now, Mr Jenner, an EHO for South Bucks District Council, has told them that wood is unhygienic and that unless the kennels are rebuilt in concrete or brick, they will not have their annual licence renewed. This will cost the Ainsworths up to £40,000, a sum they cannot afford. At nearby Taplow, Mr Jenner has given a similar ultimatum to Mrs Jane Hirer, whose kennels are both brick and timber. She says from experience that wooden kennels present fewer problems, are easier to keep clean and that the dogs find them 'a lot warmer and homelier'. As both kennels face closure, Mr Jenner says 'we are not in the business of frightening anybody. We are reasonable and are prepared to talk to them'. 'But in the end', he says, 'we are the enforcing authority'.

*   *   *

So carried away with self-importance had the EHOs now become that there seemed no limit to their zeal. Even the need to observe the law became a secondary consideration.

At 9 p.m. on a Tuesday evening in August 1992, there is a knock at the door of Ken Walker, who lives in Slough and is honorary secretary of the Wraysbury Sailing Club on a nearby gravel pit. He opens it to discover he is being served with an 'Immediate Prohibition Notice', issued by a senior EHO of the Royal Borough of Windsor and Maidenhead. The letter states, with the full authority of the Health and Safety at Work Act 1974, Sections 41(1)(b), 22, 23 and 28, that the club is henceforth 'prohibited from sailing'. It seems that on Sunday evening, two nights earlier, the EHO had arrived, unannounced, just after racing on the lake had finished for the day. The club's rescue boat had therefore been beached – but several members were still on the water, one or two without lifejackets, and others were wearing lifejackets 'which did not carry whistles'. All this made the EHO 'extremely concerned', which was why he exercised his power to stop the club sailing, on pain of fines or imprisonment, until these matters were properly rectified. When the Health and Safety at Work Act is consulted, it is seen from its preamble that its sole purpose is to secure the 'health, safety and welfare of persons at work'. It has no relevance to those who are escaping the stresses of their 'workplace' to enjoy quiet recreation in a private club on a Sunday evening. Such is the law, however, that once the prohibition notice is issued, it cannot be lifted without appeal to an industrial tribunal. In the end, it takes six months before the Wraysbury Sailing Club can legally resume sailing.

*   *   *

As 1 January 1993 approached, the disaster being inflicted on Britain's slaughterhouses by MAFF began to attract the attention of the national press. But for many abattoirs, the horrific absurdity of the MAFF regime did not become apparent until after 1 January, when the new breed of ministry-appointed veterinary officials appeared – and had to be paid for.

In Bob Newman's slaughterhouse in Farnborough in the first week of 1993, nine men are present. Three are slaughtermen, the other six are officials. The reasons for this remarkable preponderance of officials is the coming into force on 1 January of MAFF's new Fresh Meat (Hygiene and Inspection) Regulations, under which slaughterhouses must pay anything up to £60 an hour for veterinary officials to supervise their operations, in addition to the existing inspection system successfully carried out for seventy years, by local authorities. So many slaughterhouses have already closed in southern England, with the approach of the new regulatory regime, that many farmers are now having to transport their animals fifty miles or more to find one still open – like those in Farnborough and Reading. But in February 1993, Nigel Batts, chairman of the Reading abattoir, assembles his seventeen employees to tell them that their slaughterhouse too is having to close. Until a few weeks earlier the company had been doing so well that it was looking for ways to expand into new premises. But the cost of having to pay for supervision and inspection by a veterinary official with no experience of working in a slaughterhouse – adding tens of thousands of pounds a year to running costs – has made the business no longer viable. Mr Batts says that having to tell his seventeen men they are out of a job is 'the worst thing I have ever done in my life'. Another casualty of the new regulations is the deer-farming business built up over five years by Mr and Mrs Hayward at Sloper's Pond Farm, Hadley Wood, on the north edge of London. By dressing and butchering the deer themselves, they can make a modest profit by selling each carcase for £200. Now, in February 1993, they are told by the London Borough of Enfield that, under the new regulations, they too must pay veterinary fees, at a relatively modest £38.50 an hour. This, however, wipes out their profit and they have no alternative but to close down their deer farm. When agriculture ministers John Gummer and Nicholas Soames are questioned about the closure of slaughterhouses in many parts of Britain at this time, they persistently deny that this has any connection with the cost of the new regulations. The explanation provided for them by their officials, used repeatedly in the House of Commons and in letters, is that the owners, more than 200 of them, have 'taken a commercial decision not to invest in the future of their business'.

*　　*　　*

When it was taken up by the national press, this became the most celebrated 'hygiene police' story of them all – and was a turning point in waking up the public as to just how far the EHOs 'blitz' had got out of hand.

Just before Easter in April 1993, in his fourteenth century Bell Inn in the village of Aldworth on the Berkshire Downs, the landlord of many years, Ian Macaulay, is serving drinks. During a lull, he pauses to light his pipe. Shortly afterwards he is told of three people awaiting service at the other end of the bar – a man and two women. The man says, 'we've been watching you – you've been smoking behind the bar'. It turns

out he is an EHO from Newbury District Council. He warns Mr Macaulay that this constitutes a criminal offence. Two days later, a letter arrives from the council offices, by recorded delivery. Under the heading 'Food Hygiene (General) Regulations 1970', it begins, 'At midday on 2 April 1993, you were seen smoking behind the bar in the Bell and warned by health manager, Mr John Parfitt, that your conduct was a contravention of the above legislation. It is illegal for a person, engaged as a food handler, to use tobacco in a room in which there is open food'. The letter is to be treated as 'a final warning'. If Mr Macaulay is caught smoking in his own bar again, criminal proceedings will be taken against him.

*   *   *

In Oxford in the early months of 1992, the staff of Oxfam, one of Britain's largest charities, are counting with horror the cost to their funds of new regulations from the DTI on toy safety. These make it illegal to sell any toys which do not carry the CE safety mark, showing that the items have complied with safety standards laid down by the EEC. This means that charity shops like those run by Oxfam can no longer sell second-hand toys made before the CE system was introduced in 1990. Officials of the DTI claim that the Toy Safety Regulations are only implementing EEC Directive 88/378 on 'the approximation of the laws of the Member States concerning the safety of toys'. But when Oxfam examines the directive, it discovers that toys manufactured before 1990 are specifically exempted. It is only in the UK that the officials have made it a criminal offence to sell the older toys, which provide Oxfam and countless other charities with income estimated at millions of pounds a year.

*   *   *

Among the sinister features of the social workers' 'blitz' on playgroups and nursery schools was not just its totalitarian bossiness, but its heavy overlay of 'political correctness'. Here was one dedicated teacher driven to despair.

Natalie Blakely runs the Temple Close Nursery School in the Oxfordshire village of Bloxham. Like thousands of other nursery schools and playgroups in the autumn of 1993, she has been visited by social workers who have come to enforce Department of Health guidelines under the Children Act 1989. Under new requirements for staff ratios and space per child, she has had to reduce her number of children from sixty to forty. She has been instructed on 'how to keep a register, greet parents and organize the first-aid box'. She has been told to fill in a tiny pond, install new wash basins with thermostatically-controlled hot and cold taps. Her toy box, she was told, did not have enough 'black dolls or puzzles featuring black children'. Even 'the toilet rolls (with holders)' seem to be subject to the new regulations. Says Mrs Blakely, 'This school, which I have run for 25 years, ceases to be mine. I own the property only. I am emasculated. Eventually, I will close.'

*　　*　　*

Not content with shutting down hundreds of playgroups, the young social workers had now been unleashed on thousands of privately run old people's homes – with equally devastating results.

In Banbury, Ross and Barbara Greig run Fairholme House, one of Britain's 17,000 privately owned homes for the elderly and disabled which, from 1 April 1993, must undergo regular inspections by social workers under the Community Care Act 1990. In addition to the requirements already imposed by

district health authorities under the 1984 Registered Homes
Act and by EHOs under the Food Safety Act 1990 and the
Health and Safety at Work Act 1974, the home now faces
a battery of new demands from social workers. Residents'
bathwater must be kept at forty-three degrees Celsius; help-
ings of food must exceed a certain minimum; mattresses must
be turned every three days; all electrical appliances and fittings must be tested and logged under the Electricity at Work
Regulations; employees must be trained to national standards
in 'caring', 'fire prevention' and 'health and safety'. Anyone
serving food must go on a 'basic hygiene course'. There are
also now the six new sets of health and safety regulations,
under EEC directives, to be studied and complied with. But
particularly onerous are the requirements laid on homes to
comply with fire regulations, from fire escapes to safety doors.
Mrs Greig describes how, if Fairholme did not have a stair-
lift, one elderly resident 'would have to open sixteen doors
to get from her bedroom to the lounge. But we have just been
told that we must take out the stair-lift'. In general, she says,
'we are being bogged down in book-keeping and administration'. Under the ever-increasing weight of bureaucracy
which has made old peoples' homes into 'the most regulated
industry in Britain', hundreds have already closed and thousands more are expected to follow.

*   *   *

*Again the Environmental Protection Act seems dedicated to
stamping out almost any form of 'recycling'.*

In the Gloucester village of Uley, Charles Wright and Mel
Griffiths produce ale in a small local brewery. Three times a
week they shovel half a ton of spent barley out of their mash
tun, and take it by lorry ten miles to a farm on the bank of
the Severn, where Jasper Ely and Peter Smithies feed it to

their cattle and Old Spot pigs. No money changes hands because this is a friendly arrangement from which everyone benefits. But, as from 1 April 1993, under the new Waste Management Regulations, the mash becomes 'controlled waste'. The brewers will have to pay £95 for a licence to carry it. The farmer will have to pay the council £1800 for a licence to receive it. A perfect example of recycling in the rural economy will no longer make economic sense.

*　　*　　*

One of the more unpleasant by-products of the EHOs' 'hygiene blitz' was how local papers could be drawn into publicizing their activities in a way which might do immense damage to some particular business – often as it turned out, without justification. Here is a particularly tragic example.

Just outside Cheltenham, Barry and Susan Hinton have built up the Green Dragon over six years into one of the most popular country pubs in the Cotswolds, drawing praise in the national press for the quality of its food. On 16 December 1992, the bars and restaurants are packed with pre-Christmas parties, including a group of teachers from a nearby school. That evening a number of customers are taken ill with what appears to be food-poisoning. The following day, EHOs from Cotswold District Council move in, putting out statements which attract front-page attention in the local press. Most damaging is a suggestion that the cause of the illness may have been salmonella – 'It is not yet possible to identify whether this is an outbreak of salmonella', says David Stevenson, the EHO in charge of the investigation. The clamour is taken up on local radio and television and, over the next few days – which should be the busiest of the year – the Green Dragon's trade drops away almost to nothing. The Hintons receive letters from solicitors representing the teachers, demanding compensation. After several weeks when the pub has been almost empty, scientific tests show that the illness was not salmonella food-poisoning but an infection from an agent known as Norwalk virus. This may have been brought into the pub on raw mushrooms used in one of the meals. There was absolutely nothing the Hintons could have done to detect or control this virus, and environmental health officials decide not to carry their investigations any further, even though they could have checked the source of the mushrooms to determine how they became infected. But thanks to the earlier mentions of salmonella, the damage has already been done. In February 1993, while the lawyers are still arguing over thousands of pounds of compensation, Susan Hinton sends out anguished faxes to her friends and supporters – 'The Dragon is dead. Sadly, we have lost the battle against, it seems, the whole world'. Her family is in a state of 'deep shock'. The business they have given six years to building up is no more.

*   *   *

In Cheltenham, Eric Burke, the fifth generation head of a scrap business owned by his family since 1855, runs two highly-mechanized, modern yards for sorting and reclaiming metals. In November 1992, he is surprised when one of his normally reliable mechanical weighbridges twice fails tests by a Gloucestershire weights and measures inspector, even after £700 is spent on repairs. To enable it to pass, he has to spend a further £4000, replacing mechanical linkages with electronic sensors. When his other weighbridge also fails a routine test by Gloucester officials, Mr Burke has to face the prospect of spending a further £4000 on converting this instrument to electronic standard. It then comes to light that the reason his first weighbridge failed its test is because the DTI has laid down new testing procedures, which conventional 'mechanical' weighbridges cannot pass. Only bridges using electronic sensors can meet the standard. Mr Burke is reluctant to switch to the electronic system because it is less reliable and more expensive to maintain, but he accepts there is no alternative – and spends a further £2800 on new, electronic components prior to having his second instrument converted. He then learns that the DTI's new testing procedures were laid down by the Weighing Machines (Non-Automatic Weighing Machines) Regulations 1988, in anticipation of EEC Directive 90/384, which was not finalized until two years later. These procedures are not included in the directive as it is finally published, leaving the UK legislation high and dry and costing Mr Burke an unnecessary £8000.

Following a direct appeal by the Sunday Telegraph *to Mr Neil Hamilton, who was not only the Government's 'Deregulation Minister' but also the 'Weights and Measures Minister', the 1988 regulations were quickly amended and common sense was restored. Almost immediately, however, Mr Burke's scrap metal business faced two new threats, from the Environmental Protection Act 1990. Once again it seemed this was being used by the officials to stamp out all forms of recycling, in ways which threatened immense damage to the environment.*

At the beginning of 1993, like thousands of other scrapyard owners all over Britain, Mr Burke is told that, under the EPA, his company will only be allowed to operate after 1 April 1993 with a Waste Management License. The problem is not so much the £1800 cost of the licence, with an annual 'subsistence fee' of £850, as the requirement that the licence cannot be surrendered unless various conditions have been met to show that the land has not been contaminated. As the deadline approaches, Department of Environment officials have still not finalized how this is to be determined. Owners like Mr Burke are told by their banks that it will no longer be possible to value the land on which their scrapyards stand. Since the value of their yards is the main asset on which scrap dealers borrow the money necessary to finance their businesses, this threatens thousands of firms with closure. But again what is curious is that the relevant sections of the EPA are supposed to be implementing EEC Directive 91/156 on waste disposal. When the directive is examined, it appears that its purpose is to make a clear distinction between the final disposal of waste, as in landfill sites, and the recycling and reclamation of waste, which is 'desirable' and should be encouraged. In drawing up their regulations, D.o.E officials appear totally to have ignored this, and are treating metal reclamation businesses in exactly the same way as landfill sites. Despite a report from the government's Warren Spring Laboratory, which has quantified the huge environmental benefits of metal reclamation – in savings on energy and pollution – the D.o.E officials have threatened Britain's scrap industry, which earns £3 billion a year, including £1 billion-worth of exports, with the most serious crisis in its history.

* * *

But even this is not the end of Mr Burke's problems. Part of his business is based on salvaging used car batteries, for which Britain has evolved the most efficient system in Europe for their recycling, reclaiming 95 per cent; most countries fall far short of this. The key to the system lies in operations like that run by Mr Burke. All over the West Country, batteries are sent by garages to local scrapyards, where they are stored in 170 special bins supplied by Mr Burke at a cost to him of £20,000. When full, these are collected and assembled into bulk loads in Mr Burke's Cheltenham yard. They are then quickly moved on to one of only two lead-smelting works in

England, one in Yorkshire, the other in Kent. Because batteries are worth only £50 a tonne, the financial margin is tight and the profitability of the operation depends on the speed and efficiency with which they can be moved through each stage of the process. And this has been brought to such a fine art that when, in 1991, the EEC produced a 'batteries directive', 91/157, to encourage the collection and recycling of batteries, the British system might have been taken as a model. Now, however, under regulations to be brought in during 1993, under the Environmental Protection Act 1990 – supposedly to implement the Brussels directive – batteries have been classified as 'hazardous waste'. Mr Burke is told that he will have to give the county Waste Regulation Authority seventy-two hours notice each time a consignment of his 'hazardous waste' is moved, through each step of the process – and pay £15 a time. Not if they tried could the officials of the D.o.E have devised a more ingenious way of rendering the whole system both uneconomic and unworkable. It looks as though the end result of a directive designed to 'protect the environment' may simply be that millions of batteries are dumped over hedges – because no one is willing to take them.

*   *   *

Like many architects, John Evans of Newport, Gwent, is familiar with the seemingly arbitrary dictates of fire officers. He has recently had to design a sixty-room hotel. While it was being built he took enormous trouble to consult with the fire officer at every stage, and to comply with all his requirements. One of these was that bedroom doors resist fire for half an hour. Everyone agreed this should be more than adequate, since the hotel was low-rise and the bedrooms were only on the ground and first floors. Finally, the hotel is finished and everything is set for the opening festivities, widely advertised in the local press. Only days before the grand opening, the fire officer who had worked with the project retires and a new officer arrives to go through the formalities of issuing the fire certificate necessary before the hotel can open. He at once insists that all sixty bedroom doors should be taken out, and replaced with doors that are fire resistant for one hour. Not only does this cost many thousands of pounds. It means that, at enormous inconvenience to hundreds of people, the opening of the hotel has to be postponed for several weeks.

*   *   *

One of the powers given to EHOs under the Food Safety Act was that to serve 'Improvement Notices' on food handling businesses with which it becomes a criminal offence not to comply. In 1992, during the height of the 'hygiene blitz', they showered out 41,000 of these diktats. And by a strange legal quirk, they were able to use this weapon to force businesses to do things which were not actually required by law.

Near Pembroke, Mr and Mrs Robert Butterworth run the Cartref 'rest home for the elderly'. Mrs Butterworth is a State Registered Nurse, and her management team includes two other SRNs and a State Enroled Nurse. In August 1992, they are visited, unannounced, by a young woman who introduces herself as a 'Technical Assistant Environmental Health Officer' from South Pembroke District Council. She wishes to inspect the premises. In the kitchen, she observes that there is no first-aid box. 'Oh', says Mrs Butterworth, 'I think I know what you mean. My daughter had one when she was a Brownie'. The unamused official points out that it is an offence 'to run a kitchen in which a first-aid box is not installed and available'.

Mrs Butterworth reassures her that all first-aid materials are kept in the fully-stocked dispensary next door, and that she and her colleagues, as fully trained nurses, are well-qualified to use them. Six weeks later, the Butterworths receive from the council a statutory Improvement Notice, warning them that unless a first-aid box is installed in the kitchen by 1 January 1993 they will be guilty of a criminal offence, for which they can be fined and/or imprisoned for up to two years. Raising her eyebrows, Mrs Butterworth complies, buying the unnecessary first-aid box for £58. Only later does it come to light that, under Regulation 19 of the Food Hygiene (General) Regulations 1970, it is made explicitly clear that the only legal requirement is for 'first aid materials' to be available 'on the premises'. In other words, Mrs Butterworth and her nurses had been entirely within the law. But such is the nature of the Improvement Notice system that the Butterworths would have committed a criminal offence by not obeying the notice, even though it was asking for something not required by law in the first place.

*   *   *

From various towns and cities, we had reports of EHOs carrying out a 'street tidying blitz' in 1992 and 1993. Here is just one example of how power seemed to be going to their heads in this way.

Mr Eric Robinson has been placing newspaper billboards outside his newsagent's shop in East End Square, Pembroke, for twenty-six years. But in April 1993, he is told by EHOs of the South Pembroke District Council that this will no longer be tolerated. He and other traders in the town have been told that, in the interests of 'conservation' and 'the disabled', they will no longer be permitted to place any 'obstructions' on the pavements outside their shops. Greengrocers will no longer be allowed to display their fruit and vegetables. Shoe shops cannot put out racks of shoes. Newspaper placards are banned – and if the traders do not comply within two weeks,

'clean up squads' from the council's environmental health department will confiscate any item remaining.

* * *

One of the most persistent complaints against enforcement officers of all kinds was their sheer technical incompetence, the fact that they did not seem to have even the most basic practical understanding of the matters on which they were laying down the law. Here is a particularly glaring instance – the fish tanks which had to be fitted with fire extinguishers, and the poisoned dogs.

Near Pembroke is a kennels owned by an 82-year-old professional dog breeder. In January 1992, he sends off his application for renewal of his breeder's licence to South Pembroke Council, enclosing the fee of £65. He has never had any problems with his yearly renewal since licensing was introduced in 1982. But, two weeks later he receives a visit from a smartly dressed young woman who announces that, as a Technical Assistant (Animal Welfare), she has come to make an inspection. At a brisk trot, she leads the way round the premises, picking up five 'faults', saying she will return in two weeks to confirm that these have been put right. All five are rectified within half an hour of her leaving. When she returns two weeks later, she finds five more 'faults' and says she will also be sending a fire officer to inspect the premises, as there should be a fire extinguisher in each kennel. The availability of a hose and taps to fight any fire with water does not impress her. When the fire officer calls, he confirms that the taps and hosepipe are perfectly adequate and says '. . . another wasted journey she has sent me on'. He adds that he has recently been sent by the same young woman to another local business, the owner of which had been told to buy twenty fire extinguishers. The fire officer had been particularly taken by

the idea of this business, which happens to be a fish farm, 'having to install fire extinguishers for tanks of water'. Over the following months, the young official makes three more visits to the kennels, each time finding further 'faults' (which by now have cost £1500 to put right). Only on her fifth visit in the summer of 1993 is she prepared to consider renewal of the licence, although she still has five 'provisos'. One is that the sleeping boards of the kennels must be painted with creosote. When she makes this demand, she is told, 'It will be a pleasure to creosote the boards, but to whom should we send the claim?' When the animal health expert asks 'what claim', she is told 'for the vet's fees after the dogs have died of creosote poisoning'.

*　　*　　*

Few 'Euro-lunacies' were more bizarre than the various Academy of Lagado-type schemes to reduce the beef and grain mountains, and the wine and milk lakes, which had only come into being in the first place because farmers had been paid billions of pounds in subsidies to over-produce. Set-aside was another obvious example of such a scheme, to which we will return – but here is another.

Near Haverfordwest in north Pembrokeshire, Leon Downey – who used to play the viola with the Halle Orchestra – has won an international reputation as one of Britain's leading specialist cheesemakers. From his own herd of Jersey cows, he produces Llangloffan cheese. Through the Neal's Yard Dairy in London, he has customers as far afield as New York and Detroit, and he would have no trouble in selling much more than his yearly output of 30,000 lbs. But, because he uses milk from his own cows, instead of increasing production he is continually having to reduce it – three times in five years – under the EEC's system of milk quotas. The only purpose of these quotas, imposed on dairy farmers at twenty-four hours notice in 1984, is to cut down the over-production of milk in Europe. But this means that Britain, which until 1984 was self-sufficient in milk, now has to import fifteen per cent of its milk, worth hundreds of millions of pounds. No one is hit harder than Britain's specialist cheese producers, like Mr Downey. To add insult to injury, in May 1993, he receives a cheque for £198.88 from the Milk Marketing Board. This was to 'compensate' him for the tens of thousands of pounds worth of cheese he could have sold since 1988, but has not been allowed to make.

* * *

A few days after receiving his cheque, Mr Downey has a visit from Miss Rees, a young EHO with Preseli District Council. She announces that she wishes to make a 'hygiene inspection' of his dairy. As it happens, Mr Downey's premises has only recently passed with flying colours an inspection from an Agricultural Development and Advisory Service (ADAS) microbiologist, under an exacting hygiene scheme set up by the Specialist Cheese Producers' Association. But Miss Rees is not easily pleased. A few days after her visit, a letter arrives from her superior, Mr Heywood, drawing attention to twenty-two items and stating that unless Mr Downey puts matters right within thirty days he will be served with a statutory 'Improvement Notice' under the Food Safety Act, carrying the threat of fines and/or imprisonment. Careful examination shows that only three of Mr Heywood's demands actually relate to items required under the law (these include a first-aid book recording details of all accidents). But what particularly draws Mr Downey's attention is the demand that his cheese should not come into contact with wooden shelves, and that these should be covered with paint or greaseproof paper. Miss Rees, who during her visit admitted that she was unfamiliar with the technicalities of cheese production, has clearly not been aware of tests showing that paint or paper are in fact highly unhygienic for maturing cheese, because they cause a build-up of slime. Mr Downey reflects that it is a curious system which can empower those with no experience to lay down the law to professional experts – and to threaten criminal prosecution if their inappropriate advice is not followed.

*　　*　　*

Our next story touches on one of the most catastrophic bureaucratic blunders of recent years – MAFF's policy, adopted in the wake of the great 1988 salmonella scare, to enforce compulsory testing of all egg-laying flocks and the slaughter of all those found infected with salmonella. No scientific evidence was ever produced to show that salmonella in egg-laying birds ever caused food-poisoning. Bevies of distinguished scientific experts ridiculed this theory from the start. But the MAFF officials would not be budged, with the result that, between 1989 and 1993, 3.5 million birds were destroyed and 5000 egg producers were forced out of business. This had no impact on food-poisoning figures, which continued to rise. Finally, in 1993, after a report by an eminent microbiologist, Professor Heather Dick, MAFF was forced to concede that its policy had been a complete failure and the slaughter policy was abandoned. In March 1993, a parliamentary select committee reported on the treatment of the producers by MAFF, stating, 'we are astonished that MAFF should have treated so unfairly men and women already vulnerable and under extreme pressure'. It concluded, 'such maladministration as is found in this case should never be repeated'. Here is a story of just two of the farmers who lost their flocks through MAFF's compulsory slaughter programme.

Chris Brown and Barry Cheetham run two small free-range egg farms close to Mr Downey's farm. In June 1992, sixty people in Haverfordwest fall ill with salmonella food-poisoning. All the victims, it is discovered by Mr Heywood's EHOs from Preseli Council, have eaten products from a local health food shop – a quiche, coleslaw, tuna and mayonnaise, and egg sandwiches. Ever since Mrs Edwina Currie set off the great salmonella scare in December 1988, the word sal-monella has only meant one thing in the minds of EHOs – eggs. So the Preseli EHOs decide to concentrate on the egg sandwiches as the likely source of the problem. They discover that the shop's egg supplier drew on three local free-range egg farms. The flocks are tested; in two cases, traces of sal-monella are found in the chickens; and under regulations introduced in the wake of the 1988 scare, officials of MAFF slaughter both flocks. The case might seem open and shut, until we consider a number of points which come to light when an independent investigation is made. This shows, firstly, that quite a few of the victims had not eaten egg sand-wiches at all. But the health officers did not investigate any other of the products. Secondly, no evidence had been pro-duced to prove that the eggs used for the sandwiches actually came from the chickens which had been destroyed – as eggs from other sources had also been bought. Thirdly, although it was not surprising that salmonella was found in the chickens – salmonella organisms are as widespread in the environment as cold germs – none had been found in their eggs. Fourthly, even if the eggs had been infected, their hard-boiling for use in the sandwiches would have killed off the salmonella present. In short, all the evidence pointed to cross-contamination, while the various foods being handled were prepared for sale.

For Messrs Brown and Cheetham, it is too late. When they lose their flocks, they lose their livelihoods too and, because both owe money to the bank, they face ruin. In February 1993, a week after Mr Cheetham is declared bankrupt, for owing money which he only borrowed to buy his flock in the first place, the report is published by Professor Dick, which demolishes the whole basis on which MAFF has been running its slaughter policy. Within hours, the Minister of Agriculture, Mr Gummer, is forced to announce that the policy has been abandoned.

*　　*　　*

We have already seen in Selsey one disastrous consequence of the new 'fire safety' regulations concerning furniture. Here is another.

At Llandysal, Dyfed, Malcolm Headley owns a farm with ten cottages to let to holiday-makers as self-catering accommodation. He has spent much of 1992 wondering how he can afford to comply with the DTI's Furniture and Furnishings (Fire) (Safety) (Amendment) Regulations. When these come into force on 1 March 1993 they will make it a criminal offence, under the Consumer Protection Act 1987, to sell or supply to the public any upholstered furniture made between 1950 and 1988. It seems that when DTI officials published these regulations, it did not enter their heads that their provisions applied to self-catering flats and houses. But in 1990, a sharp-eyed TSO for Cornwall County Council had observed that, under the wording of the regulations, they might be applicable. When clarification was sought from the DTI, officials admitted that they had not thought of this, so they referred the matter to the LACOTS body for arbitration. LACOTS officials ruled that the new regulations should apply – which meant that the owners of Britain's 100,000 self-catering units would be faced with the task of replacing the vast majority of their beds, sofas and armchairs in little more than a year. For Mr Headley this would mean a bill for £35,000 and the trade as a whole faces costs estimated at £200 million. Since most of these operations run on very small margins, this could mean that a third or more of their owners will be forced out of business. Prolonged negotiations ensue with the DTI as a result of which, in February 1993, officials eventually offer what they consider to be a generous concession. Self-catering businesses will now be allowed an extra three years, until 31 December 1996, to comply with the law – even though it was never intended that it should apply to them in the first place.

*　　*　　*

At the Royal Welsh Show at Builth Wells in July 1992, an open-sided marquee has been erected to provide shelter for young farmers in case of rain. A fire officer instructs the show secretary that, under the regulations, the tent must be fitted with fire doors. The incredulous secretary points out that, since the marquee is open-sided, in the event of an emergency the farmers could simply walk out in any direction. The only obstacle would be the doors the official is insisting upon. Despite the insistence of the official, who claims that the organizer might decide to put walls on the marquee when he is not there, the secretary refuses to fit the doors. The official eventually accepts his point.

*　　*　　*

While the social workers were spreading havoc through Britain's nursery schools and old people's homes, some of their colleagues were promoting 'care' for their fellow human beings in a very different style.

Near Bala, Brendan McNutt, a trained social worker, owns Bryn Melyn farm, which he runs as a private childrens' home for delinquent teenagers, 'placed' with him by social services departments from all over the country. For each child the councils pay him £1800 a week, totalling £1 million a year. Mr McNutt is assisted by a staff of other qualified social workers who run the house in so relaxed a fashion that they often accompany the children on holidays to Greece, Egypt, Israel and Spain. The children are provided with a clothing allowance of £20 a week, and are lavishly provided with facilities for canoeing, fishing and riding. Some local families are paid £94 a week to house children, who appear to be under no supervision. Bala residents blame teenagers from the home for a rash of vandalism and burglaries in the town. They are appalled when the perpetrator of a violent assault on two local schoolgirls is 'punished' by being sent off to 'swim with dolphins'. When asked about the apparently astronomic cost to public funds for sending teenagers to Bryn Melyn, an official of Liverpool City Council, one of the social services departments which does so, will only observe, 'It is not unusual to pay £1800 a week for accommodation in a secure unit'. This equates to twice the cost of a double room at the Ritz Hotel in London.

*   *   *

In Llanrwst in May 1993, the work of the nine employees of the Conwy Valley Meat Company is disrupted for a month by building works required to enable the slaughterhouse to comply with MAFF's interpretation of the Fresh Meat (Hygiene and Inspection) Regulations 1992. Officials have told the abattoir owner that he must cease trading until the ceiling is raised by six feet. The works cost £20,000.

*   *   *

Here, a concern for 'safety' and 'environment' combine to produce a wonderfully insane solution to a non-existent problem.

In Herefordshire, Richard Green, who rears poultry and grows blackcurrants, has like many other farmers a small private petrol tank to supply his farm vehicles. In February 1993, he is informed by his local fire officer that a new method has been introduced to test such tanks for any leakage. For decades, this sort of testing has been carried out by injecting inert gas into the tank and measuring any loss of pressure. But now the Health and Safety Executive's Hazardous Installation Branch has decided that, because of one tiny incident where a cap lifted off, it would be safer to test by a different method, which involves filling the tank with water. The problem is that this not only contaminates the petrol tank with water, it also pollutes hundreds of gallons of water with minute quantities of petrol. Under the Environmental Protection Act 1990, this becomes 'hazardous waste' which can only be disposed of by an authorized contractor at a 'designated site'. In Mr Green's case, this means that his contaminated water must be taken 200 miles to Rayleigh in Essex. It will cost him £650.

* * *

Near Bridgnorth, Clem Shaw, a 67-year-old poultry farmer, keeps what is believed to be the only commercial flock of pure-bred Wyandottes left anywhere in Europe or America. Forty years ago, this breed was one of the most popular in the world. But it has been vanishing so fast that when, a few years back, a senior poultry vet from ADAS, then part of MAFF, came upon Mr Shaw's flock, he was tremendously excited. It was a gene pool of immense value. But, for three years, Mr Shaw has been locked in a battle with MAFF over its compulsory inspection and slaughter programme intro-

The Famous
WYANDOTTE
EGG

duced in the wake of the great salmonella scare. His fear is that, if any of his priceless birds are found to be infected, his flock's days will be numbered. In November 1992, MAFF officials finally get him into court for offences related to their salmonella policy. He is found guilty on three of four charges. But he immediately appeals and when he is then found not guilty of a second offence, he appeals again. He is determined to spin out the legal process as long as possible, convinced that, if he loses, he runs the risk of the whole flock eventually having to be slaughtered. And if the last White Wynadotte flock in the western world is to be wiped out, Mr Shaw is determined that he will perform the awful task himself.

* * *

Also in Bridgnorth is the headquarters of the Severn Valley Railway, where a particular highlight for the tens of thousands of visitors each year is a tour of the engine shed, to examine the steam locomotives at close quarters. But in the summer of 1992, they are shocked to see notices explaining that public entry to the engine shed is no longer permitted. The volunteers who run the railway have to explain that this is because of a ruling by an official of the Health and Safety Executive. There has never been any accident or possibility of danger but such are the HSE's powers to serve statutory notices under the Health and Safety at Work Act that the Railway believes it has no alternative but to exclude the public.

* * *

Another victory for the social workers – closing down one of the oldest prep schools in the country, for no reason whatsoever. Many boarding schools had trouble at this time with 'politically correct' social workers who had obviously never seen such institutions before. When they arrived at Eton, the only thing they could find to recommend was that 'hoods' should be fitted over the house telephones so that if the boys wished to complain to their parents about the way they were being treated, their conversations could not be overheard.

Near Rugby, Warwickshire, the Dunchurch-Winton prep school is looking forward to celebrating its 125th anniversary in the summer of 1993. In 1992, despite the strains of the recession which have hit all private schools, three pupils have won scholarships to the neighbouring public school at Rugby. All seems well until the school begins receiving visits from Warwickshire social workers, using new powers granted them under the Children Act 1989. Because the boarding roll has fallen just below fifty – the cut-off point for the application of the Act – social workers can treat Dunchurch-Winton as if it was a 'children's home' – which is how they persist in describing the school, to the considerable irritation of its joint headmasters, Sandy Marshall and Arne Olsen.

The two members of the 'social work team' most involved are a woman who insists on being addressed as 'Ms Gloria' and a male colleague who wears sandals without socks. Relations begin to sour during the summer holidays when, following an incident in which a member of staff had slapped a boy for bullying, social workers go round the homes of local boarders, interrogating them about the staff's drinking habits and possible sexual improprieties. Although nothing comes to light, the school awaits the formal report of the social workers with foreboding. When it arrives at the beginning of 1993, it orders the school to carry out major capital expenditure on refurbishing dormitories, and the installation of new washing and toilet facilities. The cost of these works is £30,000, much more than the school can afford. Sadly, the headmasters and the governors conclude that at the end of the summer term, instead of celebrating its 125th birthday, the school will have to close altogether.

*   *   *

Another classic instance of how 'guidance' notes were treated as if they were a legal requirement. This one probably cost public bodies and private organizations upwards of £100 million before, in the summer of 1993, the racket was first exposed in the Sunday Telegraph. *But it still continues to claim many victims.*

At Stratford-on-Avon, Joyce Hudson is the head of a state school for disabled children. In June 1992, like the heads of other state schools in Warwickshire, she is summoned to a meeting to be told how it is now necessary for all schools to comply with the Electricity at Work Regulations 1989. They must each be prepared, at short notice, to assemble all the electricity appliances in their schools in one room, to be tested and logged by a qualified electrician who has been hired by the council on a two-and-a-half year contract for the purpose. Apart from the disruption this will cause, it will cost the county's education budget up to £50,000. Of course, Warwickshire schools are not alone. Other schools, hotels, old people's homes and countless businesses, all over Britain, have been told either by public officials or by private contractors and consultants that the testing and logging of plugs and electrical equipment is compulsory, and that failure to comply could lead to fines up to £20,000. Yet, when the Electricity at Work Regulations are examined, it turns out that these things are not required by law at all. The regulations merely say that 'all systems should be maintained ... as far as is reasonably practical'. Only in the accompanying memorandum of 'guidance', prepared by the Health and Safety Executive, does it state that 'regular inspection is essential', that this must be done by a 'qualified person' and that 'without records of maintenance' it 'cannot be certain that the requirement for maintenance has been complied with'. Once again millions of pounds are being spent to comply not so much with regulations as with 'guidance notes' which have no force in law.

* * *

In Birmingham, R.E.V. Gomm Ltd have a small workshop for badge enamelling, which involves the use of small amounts of lead. In October 1991, they were visited by officials of the Health and Safety Executive who took blood samples from female staff. Although lead levels found were well within safety limits, the company was instructed to suspend two members of staff on full pay for six months, including the manageress, because both were pregnant. The HSE ordered the firm to fit extractors and to carry out works to the walls and floor of the workshop, even though these had only recently been refurbished. In 1992, after the case had been taken up by the local MP and by a minister at the Department of Employment, the firm is told that its workshop has been reclassified as only 'a marginal lead user'. The suspended employees can return to work. But there is no compensation for the unnecessary works carried out to the building, nor for the thousands of pounds spent on wages to keep the two employees at home.

* * *

Near Sutton Coldfield, a factory owned by Whale Tankers stands next to a canal owned by the British Waterways Board. Any rain falling on the factory roof is discharged via gutters into the canal. In 1992, Whale receives a letter from the BWB stating that, under a new charging scheme instituted by the National Rivers Authority, Whale will in future have to pay

£4800 a year for allowing its water to drain into the canal, or find some 'alternate method of disposal'. When the BWB is asked how such a sum can be justified, it replies that the charge is necessary because Whale's rainwater 'contributes to the erosion of the system'.

*   *   *

A frequent complaint from businessmen and consultants all over Britain was how officials from the DTI seemed to see their chief function as being to hinder trade and close down industry. Here is a poignant example.

In Tamworth, Staffordshire, in February 1993, Dr Philip Rose, managing director of ACE, a small engineering firm, is anxiously awaiting a message from officials in the DTI, knowing that if it does not arrive within days, his company will go bankrupt. In December 1989, ACE signed contracts to supply a factory in Russia with equipment to make tennis racquets and fishing rods with carbon fibre epoxy, for sale to the West. By December 1990, with the full approval of HM Customs and Excise, ACE had completed three shipments. But in May 1991, without warning, a fourth shipment was seized by customs officials. Furthermore, in a dawn raid on Dr Rose's home, they arrested him in front of his children and carried out a rigorous search of his home, even searching the linings of his jacket pockets.

The officials had somehow formed the impression that the carbon fibre equipment ACE was supplying to the Russians to make rods and racquets could also be used for making 'rocket parts'. In October 1991, HM Customs dropped their threat of prosecution and returned the seized goods – but only on condition that Dr Rose paid £100,000 because the export of such 'strategically sensitive' materials without a licence was prohibited. At a meeting with the trade minister,

Tim Sainsbury, Dr Rose tried to explain that his equipment, designed to make 'cheap and cheerful' carbon fibre for sports goods could have no conceivable strategic value. Technically, it was light years away from the aerospace-grade material used in rockets (which is so difficult to manufacture that no UK firm has the technical facilities to do it). Still no licence was forthcoming, and then in April 1992, in the wake of the Gulf War, ACE learned that the real objection to its exporting to Russia came from the Ministry of Defence, which feared that the equipment might be converted there to military use, this time for 'sale to Iraq'. Ten months later, by which time Dr Rose had won strong support from the British Embassy in Moscow, for his efforts to increase Britain's trade with Russia, he is granted another ministerial interview, this time with the procurement minister at the MOD, Jonathan Aitken.

MOD officials still maintain that his equipment could be 'tweaked up' for military purposes, although now for 'sale to Iran'. Dr Rose accepts that his contract is virtually in ruins. ACE will go into liquidation unless a final appeal to local MP David Lightbown, a government whip, and press publicity in the *Sunday Telegraph*, can do the trick. On 6 March 1993, word comes through that the licence has been granted in the nick of time. There is just one tiny snag. As well as the main licence, officials have decided that ACE requires an additional permit for some sheet moulding equipment. In July, following a further intervention by Mr Aitken, even this is granted. But officials then pull their master stroke. The whole matter must now be referred to COCOM, a mysterious body in Paris which was set up at the height of the cold war to vet the export of strategic materials to the Soviet Union. The fact that the Cold War has been over for three years and that the Soviet Union no longer exists is irrelevant to the DTI officials. Dr Rose must be prevented at all costs from helping the Russians to make those tennis racquets and fishing rods.

* * *

Again, the Environmental Protection Act is seen inflicting devastation on British industry. Many companies like this one were forced either to lay off men or close down altogether – for no environmental gain whatsoever.

In Burslem, Stoke-on-Trent, Bert Adams runs a small company making heat-resistant refractory linings for furnaces, boilers and incinerators. In November 1992 he receives a letter from the Director of Housing and Health of the Stoke City Council requiring him to register his manufacturing process under the Environmental Protection Act 1990, for which there will be a fee of £800. The council refers to the Environmental Protection (Prescribed Processes and Substances) Regulations 1991, Section 3.6, on 'ceramic production', which requires processes involving the firing of refractory goods in a kiln to be registered.

In his reply to the council, Mr Adams points out that there appears to be a misunderstanding. His company does not use a kiln. It makes its refractory linings by a wet process, similar to that for making concrete. The whole purpose of the regulations cited is to control air pollution. His process does not involve any measurable emissions to air. This being so, he writes, his process does not require registration. Council officials, however, do not seem to understand the point. In reply they merely state that they have asked the D.o.E for a ruling as to the definition of 'refractory goods', irrespective of the fact that, under the definition already provided by the regulations, Mr Adams' process is clearly exempted from the need to register.

This is not the first time that Mr Adams' company has had

problems with the Environmental Protection Act. So severe are the conditions of use applied to the incinerators he makes that, under another part of the Act, his customers are being forced to fit up to £20,000-worth of monitoring equipment – the same sort of equipment fitted to huge municipal incinerators – to units which he sells for around £3000. Not surprisingly, his customers – who included schools, local authorities, hospitals and vets – can no longer afford to buy his incinerators. This has lost Mr Adams some £100,000 in annual turnover, and he has had to make half his workforce redundant – six men 'who will probably never be re-employed'.

* * *

Another widespread complaint against enforcement officials of all kinds was the way they went for 'responsible' individuals or firms, while leaving the real problem cases untouched. This was certainly true of the new Child Support Agency, which seemed to find it easier to harry thousands of fathers who had already made responsible financial arrangements for their families rather than chase down those fathers who had disappeared without making any provision at all.

In Chester in August 1993, solicitor Susan Deas is preparing a test case against the new Child Support Agency. After a few months in operation, it is clear that this is causing havoc among countless parents and children from broken homes. Mrs Deas' client, Gary Crozier, is a manual worker from Carlisle who divorced in 1986. Like many fathers, he signed over the ownership of the marital home to his wife, in return for relinquishing any further financial responsibility for his son. But the Child Support Agency does not recognize such arrangements, even though they may have been made with the full support of a court. Mr Crozier, who has since re-married, is now being ordered by agency officials to pay £37

a week maintenance for his son. The case is being watched closely by other lawyers and their clients in similar situations all over Britain, who share a sense of injustice at the way the agency's financial demands seem to bear no relationship to the ability of fathers to pay. One father in London has been left with only £18 a week to live on.

*   *   *

In Kirkby, Merseyside, car worker John Jones and his wife Veronica have for more than twenty years kept a small pet monkey, Margo. The animal lives with them 'like one of the family' and 'likes nothing better than to sit in front of the telly with a plate of curry and chips'. But in June 1993, EHOs of Knowsley Council rule that, as a Macaque, Margo comes under the Dangerous Animals Act and that, if the Joneses wish to keep her, they must fit every window in their house with reinforced double glazing. This will cost many thousands of pounds, more than the Joneses can afford, so they are forced to say goodbye to their harmless pet. A council spokesman explains 'we are acting on the advice of a vet who has confirmed that Margo is classed as a dangerous wild animal'.

*   *   *

Another example of how we could no longer look to the courts to curb the excesses of the officials.

The Abbeyfield Society is a Christian housing association with 1000 independent houses all over the country, where small groups of people can live together in a homely setting, sharing domestic chores. In 1991, EHOs began calling on a number of these virtually private homes, announcing that, under the Food Safety Act 1990, they must now be treated as 'food businesses' and are therefore subject to all the regulations applying to restaurants and other catering establishments.

When an EHO from Salford City Council walked into the kitchen of a home in Walkden, run by the Abbeyfield Worsley Society, his first action was to throw a wooden cutting board and rolling pin into the bin, saying 'these aren't allowed' – despite protests from the owner that they had been a wedding present many years before.

What followed was a battery of statutory Improvement Notices served on the home by the council, including a ruling that residents could not work in the kitchen without special protective clothing. The society protested that this was not in the spirit of what was essentially a private home, and went to court – where the magistrates ruled that the requirements should apply only to paid staff. But this so incensed the 'hygiene police' that, at huge expense, they took the case to the High Court in London.

Now, in March 1993, two learned judges – Mr Justice Rose and Mr Justice Waller – spend the best part of a day arguing at interminable length over such points as whether a bottle of milk should, within the meaning of the hygiene regulations, be regarded as an 'open' or 'covered' food. Is it still a 'covered' food, when you have taken off the foil cap? asks one. Their final judgement of Solomon is that the octogenarian residents of the Abbeyfield home may be permitted to peel vegetables or make tea in their ordinary, everyday clothes. But if they want to butter scones (butter being an 'open' food), they must put on special overalls. These legal niceties are all so confusing to the residents that, even though they would still like to help in the kitchen, they are now frightened to do so lest they might do something 'against the regulations'.

*   *   *

Yet another example of how the Environmental Protection Act is helping to close down British industry.

In Oldham, Polymeric Labels, a company launched in 1986 to market a process for printing on rubber, has a record of which any Conservative government should be proud. Seven years ago, British rubber companies were being supplied almost entirely from Italy. Now Polymeric has won ninety per cent of the UK market, and is rapidly increasing its exports all round the world. So impressed is the DTI by this achievement that it has offered the company a grant of £45,000 to expand further. But in July 1993 the firm is told by Oldham Council's environmental health department that, because its manufacturing process emits 'solvents' at a rate equivalent to one tin of creosote or paint a week per employee, it is nearing the threshold laid down under EEC Directive 84/360 where it must become a 'prescribed process' under the Environmental Protection Act 1990. If this happens, the company will have to spend so many hundreds of thousands of pounds on 'pollution abatement equipment' that it may have to close down. Friendly advice from the EHOs is that it would be 'better not to expand any further'.

*   *   *

Another good example of the courts upholding a quite bizarre prosecution by the officials – although in this case, it seemed that even the officials eventually accepted they had gone too far.

In Bolton, Lancashire, in June 1990, a young woman walks into the bakery run by Mrs Dorothy Wood, introducing herself with the words, 'I've got the power to close down businesses like this'. She is an EHO from Bolton Metropolitan District Council. She inspects the bakery three times in six months, and then Mrs Wood hears nothing more for a year until, in March 1992, she receives summonses to appear before the local magistrates on ten criminal charges under the Food Hygiene (General) Regulations 1970. Mrs Wood is

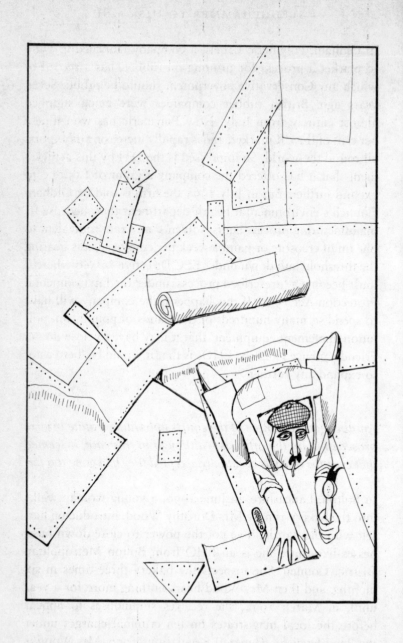

astonished at the nature of some of the charges. A box of butter has been found in the same refrigerator as a sealed packet of meat. The edge of a table, used to hold buckets of raw potatoes ready for peeling, had been 'chipped'. The ceiling of a cellar-room, which had long been out of use, was 'rough'. A bucket of 'stagnant water' was hot water being used to clean the floor.

The court hearing lasts two days, during which the magistrates refuse to allow expert defence evidence from a professional consultant. They find Mrs Wood guilty on all counts, and she is fined £2000. A disbelieving Mrs Wood appeals against the four charges she considers most outrageous. Shortly before these are due to be heard in the Crown Court in September 1992, she is told that the council has decided 'not to offer any evidence'. The court quashes all ten convictions and sends Mrs Wood a cheque for £2000.

* * *

In Blackburn, the Cavalier Carpet Company has been looking in astonishment at the £28 billion a year cost to EEC taxpayers of the Common Agricultural Policy. They calculate that it would be considerably cheaper to cover every square inch of the twelve EEC countries with top-quality carpet.

* * *

In Preston in September 1992, the local health authority is advertising vacancies in its 'dynamic and active Health Promotion Unit' for new staff to work on 'HIV/Aids' related projects. These 'will work closely with the HIV/Aids Administrator, the HIV/Aids Prevention Coordinator, the HIV/Aids Trainer and a number of other key agencies within the district'. At the time when business closures in the private sector are at record levels, Preston is the only one of many authorities recruiting in the HIV/Aids field. In North Mersey they

are looking for a 'Senior Health Promotion Officer to promote HIV, Aids and Sexual Health for Black and Racial Min-
ority Groups'. In London, the 'West London Health
Promotion Agency' is looking for an 'HIV Prevention Officer'
to 'develop HIV prevention work responsive to the needs
of "People With Learning Difficulties"'. In Newcastle, even
housing associations must have their own 'Tenant Support
Workers (HIV and Aids)'. As the army of HIV/Aids officials
grows ever larger, it is observed that these may soon out-
number those actually suffering from the disease.

*   *   *

*In 1993, Britain's hundreds of trading standards officers were
costing the country upwards of £100 million a year as they
carried out their 'blitz' under regulations intended to implement EEC directives. Meanwhile, to enforce the same directives in Italy, there were only eight TSOs in the whole
country.*

In Blackpool, David Halsall Plc are one of Britain's biggest
importers of toys. They sell 200,000 toys a day, worth £20
million a year. Whenever they place a new toy on the market,
they first have it checked for safety by local TSOs. But there
are no guarantees that a toy passed by TSOs in one area will
not meet with objections from those in another – as happens
in 1992 with two types of 'memory gel' toy imported from
the Far East. First some 'Spikey Sticky Balls' are suspended
from sale by TSOs in Trafford. Then the company is prosecuted by TSOs in Newcastle-on-Tyne for selling 'Kung Fu
Sticky Balls'. The charge is brought under the Food Imitations
(Safety) Regulations 1989, implementing EEC Directive 87/
357 which concerns products which 'appearing to be other
than they are, endanger the safety of consumers'. The regulations which the officials claim have been infringed make it

a criminal offence to offer for sale any goods which 'are not food but which have a form, odour, colour, appearance, packaging or labelling, volume or size which is likely to cause persons, in particular children, to confuse them with food'. The key phrase here, according to lawyers for the company, is '*likely* to confuse'. The prosecution will have to prove that the jelly-like toys are so like food that children could easily be confused. The company therefore commissions an eminent paediatrician, Professor T.J. David of the University of Manchester, to carry out extensive tests with a range of children of all backgrounds and ages between two and fourteen, to see whether they are likely to mistake the toys for food.

In the first of the professor's tests, on 'Spikey Sticky Ball Toys', each of 182 children are asked to 'hold the toy, say what he or she thinks it is and finally whether he or she would eat it'. 113 are puzzled as to how to describe the object, but the largest sub-group identify it as some sort of 'ball', their descriptions ranging from 'a slime thing', 'horrible', 'one of them things you throw', to 'a bomb' and 'you kill people with it'. In answer to the question 'would you eat it?', all 182 children answer 'no'. On the 'Kung Fu and Splatt Balls', 204 children are tested. Sixteen reply 'ball', nine say 'slime', one says 'disgusting' and twenty-two include the word 'jelly' in their answer. This time, eight children – four per cent – say they 'might' eat the ball. But Professor David concludes from his tests that the children are not 'likely' to confuse the toys with food. The company plans to cite this expert evidence when the case against the Kung Fu Balls is heard by Newcastle magistrates.

Before this happens, however, in December 1992, the company receives from the DTI a 'Prohibition Notice', signed by Baroness Denton, the under-secretary for 'Consumer Affairs and Small Firms', stating that the 'articles known as Jelly Balls, being a spherical elastic jelly-like product' are 'unsafe', and that it will be a criminal offence for David Halsall Plc to sell them, punishable by imprisonment and/or a fine 'not exceeding £5000'. The offence is no longer, as stated by the regulations, that the toys are 'likely' to be confused with food, but simply that they 'could' be so confused, meaning that even one child would be enough. The officials of the DTI do not have to give any reasons for their ruling, and there is no appeal against it.

In July 1993, the case of the 'Jelly Balls' finally comes before Newcastle magistrates, who agree that children are not 'likely' to confuse the balls with food and throw the case out. This means that local shops are again free to sell the toys, but the company, under the DTI's Prohibition Notice, are no longer allowed to supply them. The Notice still remains in force, and there is no way the company can challenge it.

*　　*　　*

No example of the National Rivers Authority's new drive to increase its income could have been more bizarre than this – the woman who was charged for collecting rainwater (see also the stories under 'Stoke Gabriel' and 'Sutton Coldfield' where users were charged for precisely the opposite, not keeping their rainwater). But, as the story goes on to show, this was not the only way officials had discovered to make money out of the owners of Britain's two million private water supplies – even if they had to misuse an EEC directive to do it, in a way applied nowhere else in Europe.

The Kirkstone Pass Hotel run by Mrs Pat Yates, 1500 feet up a Lakeland mountainside, is almost the highest pub in England. It is also only a few miles from the place with the highest rainfall in England – and herein lies the beginning of a problem for Mrs Yates, for just behind the pub she has a tank in which she catches a tiny amount of the rainwater

which streams down the surrounding hillsides. The NRA, noting this, have sent her a bill for £25 for 'use' of the rain-water. Mrs Yates protests that 'it is God's rain. I cannot see how they have the nerve to charge me for it'. But the NRA's reply is, 'we are the guardians of water', explaining that if Mrs Yates didn't catch the water it would flow down the hill into the river system, where it would be 'available to be used by someone'.

Meanwhile in Tillingham, Essex, Mr Brien Symes is being informed by the NRA that he must pay more than £2000 to use water from a small underground stream for a watercress bed and irrigation of his crops. This stream flows straight on to the sea nearby. Thus the NRA charges Mrs Yates for using water which might otherwise be used by someone else whereas Mr Symes is charged for using water which no one else could be in a position to use.

But this is not the end of Mrs Yates' problem with water. She also has to pay her local council an annual charge of nearly £1000 for the water she collects from the mountainside to be tested and analysed seven times a year, to ensure that it is pure enough to be fit for drinking. This is obligatory under the Private Water Supplies Regulations 1991, brought in to comply with the EEC's so-called 'drinking water' direc-tive. Yet, when the annexes of the directive are examined, it appears that it is only concerned to require testing more than once a year of supplies which are regularly used by more than 10,000 people.

*　　*　　*

Another particularly sad case of the havoc caused by MAFF's brutal enforcement of its new meat hygiene regulations.

Mrs Jean Jackson and her husband run a small craft slaugh-terhouse serving top quality beef to hotels and restaurants all over the Lake District. They also provide the only 'casualty' service for the whole of Cumbria, and even over the border into Scotland – that is to say they are available to come out whenever a farmer has an animal injured on the farm. In 1992, faced with the complex structural requirements needed to bring their premises to 'full EEC standard' required by MAFF's new Fresh Meat (Hygiene and Inspection) Regulations, implementing EEC Directive 91/497, the Jacksons conclude that they will have to build a completely new abattoir costing £1 million – which they will not be able to finish before 1995.

In the meantime, they ask the ministry if they can continue in business with their existing premises. MAFF officials reply that they can do this only if they spend £20,000 on improvements to their present slaughterhouse, far more than they hope to make back in the two years it will take to move to the new premises. While they are still debating with the ministry, in January 1993, the Jacksons are hit by the other part of the regulations, the crippling cost of the new veterinary inspections. In April they find that they can no longer afford to continue in business. Cumbria loses its last high-quality, craft slaughterhouse, and farmers for forty miles around lose their last 'casualty' service.

*　　*　　*

It was not only the overzealous enforcement of 'hygiene' regulations by EHOs which was inflicting untold damage on Britain's food industry. Even the regulations themselves were in chaos, as this story shows.

In Grasmere, Ambleside, Reg Gifford owns Michael's Nook, a well-known country house hotel. When this was converted, he took great care to retain the original ambience of the house, including the traditional kitchen fittings. Nevertheless, he installed two refrigerators, in addition to an outside cold store. These were quite sufficient for the hotel's needs, since most of the food – for which the hotel has a high reputation – is made, cooked and served soon after purchase. In 1992, however, Mr Gifford becomes aware of the Department of Health's new Food Hygiene (Amendment) Regulations 1990 and 1991, made under the Food Safety Act 1990. Introduced as part of the Government's response to the 1988 salmonella scare, these require some of the foods Mr Gifford serves to be kept at 5°C. In order to comply with this requirement, he needs to fit new, high-performance refrigerators, for which major building alterations are needed, involving the construction of a new room. With equipment, the modifications cost him £25,000.

Mr Gifford is not alone in having to spend large sums at this time – the height of the 'deepest recession in living memory' – to comply with the 5°C temperature requirement. One trade estimate puts the sum spent by hotels, shops and other food-handling businesses at '£100 million'. In February 1993, however, only weeks before the new regulations are due to take effect, on 1 April 1993, officials of the D.o.H announce that the regulations are to be 'reviewed' and will therefore not be implemented. It seems that hundreds of thousands of businesses, like Mr Gifford's, have spent the £100 million in vain.

*   *   *

In July 1993, Mr and Mrs Beecroft of Leighton Buzzard are staying at a hotel in the Lake District. At dinner, Mrs Beecroft asks for a rare steak and is astonished to be told that this can only be supplied if she is first prepared to 'sign the order'. When she asks why, she is told that this has been insisted on by an EHO, 'under EEC regulations', as 'the meat would be insufficiently cooked to destroy injurious bacteria'. In complying with this remarkable instruction, the management is probably unaware that (a) it has nothing to do with regu-

lations from the EEC; (b) it has nothing to do with any other regulations; and (c) it has nothing whatsoever to do with hygiene. Meat is inherently one of the safest forms of food, and the only risk comes from surface contamination which would be dealt with by the cooking of even the rarest steak. The EHO has only been demonstrating that he is an officious ass. But possibly the hoteliers have been so terrified that he might find some reason for closing them down that they did not dare to argue.

*   *   *

Near Appleby, Westmoreland, Roger Brown runs a small horticultural nursery selling garden plants. He has been using a small disused quarry on his land to deposit leaves and old compost. He is notified by the Waste Regulation Inspector (North) of Cumbria County Council that, because the compost is a by-product of his commercial activity, it now comes under the Environmental Protection Act 1990 and constitutes 'controlled waste'. He is told that the County Solicitor is considering legal action to stop him dumping it on his own land.

Mr Brown is then notified by the Site Licensing and Industrial Waste Officer that 'continued deposits of such waste without relevant permission may not only result in prosecution for breach of Section 3 of the 1974 Control of Pollution Act, but also additional expense in removal of waste'. Because of the inaccessible nature of the quarry, Mr Brown discovers that it will cost him £20,000 to have the compost removed by an authorized contractor, a sum which would mean the closure of his business. When he points this out to the officials, he is informed that the county council will 'have no alternative' but to commence legal proceedings. Only when the case is taken up by Mr Brown's MP does the County Solicitor rule that the compost does not constitute 'controlled waste' after all. The Site Licensing and Industrial Waste Officer writes to say 'please accept my apologies for any concern these events may have caused'.

Mr Brown, who features in this story, was not the only person who faced prosecution under the EPA for keeping a compost heap. But, following a similar case in Sussex involving a landscape gardener, the officials of the D.o.E changed the regulations. Nevertheless, it still remained a criminal offence to remove cuttings, leaves or branches if these were produced by someone else's gardening activities, and it was illegal to take compost or manure from a neighbour's garden unless one had a Waste Carriers' License (£95) and the final recipient had a Waste Management License (£1800).

*   *   *

Not the least curious feature of the 'blitz' launched by social workers on privately run old people's homes in 1993 was the way this brought to light a double standard. As with the privately run playgroups, many social workers seemed to imagine that any privately managed concern must be run only 'to make money'. They often therefore displayed a particular animus against the private concerns, applying much more rigorous standards than were expected in care homes run by social services departments themselves. What made this particularly significant was that the private homes were now also made dependent on the social services departments for many of their 'placements' of old people, and the funding that went with them − residents who might otherwise be sent to the social services own homes.

The town of Millom has two old people's homes. St George's is privately owned and run by Leo and Polly Kirk, who between them have seventy years experience of nursing and caring for others. Down the road is Lapstone House, owned and run by Cumbria Social Services Department. In the summer of 1993, many privately run nursing homes – which employ half a million people – are facing a crisis. Thousands may have to close because they cannot afford to meet the onerous new 'registration' standards imposed on them by social workers. Furthermore, under the Community Care Act 1990, since 1 April 1993 they have been in competition for funds and 'placements' with homes run by the social workers themselves, to which the same exacting standards do not seem to apply.

As it happens, the two homes in Millom are a good example of this because, in the summer of 1993, both have recently been inspected by the Cumbria Social Services Inspectorate. The report on St George's shows that it cannot be faulted. But when the social services came to inspect the home run by their own council, they had to admit that 'many of the bedrooms do not meet the minimum size which would be required for registration' and some residents had to buy their own bedding. Decoration was of 'a very poor standard'. There were not enough bathrooms. Toilets were 'antiquated'. Furthermore, the inspectors found that 'there is no indication that there is any particular person in charge at night'. On at least six points the council home had not met requirements which social workers now insist on in private homes. Had it been privately owned, Lapstone House would have been forced to close. Yet not only is it permitted to continue, it receives taxpayers' money for each resident, equivalent to £314 a week. Payments for each resident of the privately owned home are limited, under the Community Care Act, to £220.

* * *

A particularly sad example of the damage done by overzealous social workers.

At Allonby, looking over the Solway Firth, the Sunshine Children's Home in Scalesceugh Hall has been providing seaside holidays for small groups of children from poor homes, every year since 1933. Thousands of children have benefited from these holidays, including many sent by local authorities. The home has always been staffed by a team of responsible volunteers. But, early in 1993, social workers from Cumbria County Council, using new powers under the Children Act 1989, rule that this can no longer be permitted. As a 'childrens' home' under the Act, the Sunshine Home must be staffed by 'properly trained professionals'. Since this is contrary to the whole basis on which the home has operated, and there is no way the charity which owns it has sufficient funds to comply with the social workers' ruling, it is announced that the Sunshine Home will not be reopening at Easter 1993. For the first time in sixty years, it has had to close.

*　　*　　*

Early in 1993, the social workers of the Borders Regional Council draw up guidelines under which they are proposing to enforce their supervision of privately owned old people's homes. The homes cannot be registered unless they permit sexual relationships between residents, including homosexual relationships, and 'the proprietors must provide a counselling service if such relationships break down'.

*　　*　　*

On Deeside, Ian Alcock is a former City stockbroker who now runs his own 500-acre organic hill farm. He and his wife Diana have decided that when in due course they die, they would like to be buried on a particularly beautiful hilltop on the farm, designated as a Site of Special Scientific Interest because of its rare orchids. When he enquired of the local Kincardine and Deeside Council whether there would be any problem with this, he found himself locked in a lengthy battle with planning officials who not only take an enormous amount of time but cost him £197 in planning fees. Eventually he appeals to the Scottish Office in Edinburgh which, in December 1992, rules that since private graves on the Aboyne farm do not constitute 'a change of land use', and since digging the graves does not 'constitute an engineering project' under the Town and Country Planning Regulations, no planning permission is in fact required.

* * *

This is a small but particularly glaring example of how the UK government was often much more zealous in implementing EEC directives than other Member States.

Oyster farmers in the clear waters along the lovely coast of Argyll are informed by the Scottish Office in the autumn of 1992 of new regulations affecting them, under EEC Directive 91/492, 'laying down health conditions for the production and placing on the market of live bivalve molluscs'. The directive orders that all coastal waters in the EEC should be classified from A to E, and that shellfish may only be sold freely from waters found to be of the 'A standard' of cleanliness. Preliminary tests show that only half the oyster farms on the Argyll coast are likely to come out as Class A (and the Scottish Office refuses to allow any independent analysis). This greatly alarms the oyster farmers, since it threatens to drive several of them out of business. But their alarm soon changes to considerable anger when they learn that not only all the oyster sites in France have been given the A classification, but also all those in the Netherlands. Most of the Dutch oyster beds

are situated around the delta of the Rhine, the most heavily polluted waterway in Europe.

*   *   *

It might seem hard to imagine anywhere in the UK likely to be more remote from the dead hand of officialdom than the islands of the Outer Hebrides – although since 1991, British television viewers have become familiar with the grim concrete headquarters of the Western Isles Council in Stornoway, where officials lost the astronomic sum of £23 million belonging to local charge-payers by depositing it with the collapsed Middle Eastern Bank, BCCI. The loss accounted for an increase in the Western Isles rates from a £26-a-head poll tax in 1992 to a council tax on a D-band property in 1993 of £898 – the largest individual tax increase ever recorded in British history. But this was not the only evidence that mad officials were at work in the Hebrides.

In the autumn of 1992, a large brown envelope is received by the organizers of a small childrens' playgroup on the island of North Harris – two dozen or so Gaelic-speaking children gathered from the island's scattered crofts to meet in a small community hall. The envelope, from the Western Isles Council Social Services Department, contains 'Draft Guidance for the Registration of Day Care for Children Under Eight Provided Outwith Domestic Premises', under the Children Act 1989. The document also notifies the organizers that they must take cognizance of the Race Relations Act 1976, the Disabled Persons Act 1975, the Health and Safety at Work Act 1974; the Food Safety Act 1990; and the Food Hygiene (Scotland) Regulations 1959–78.

The playgroup organizers read in amazement through twenty pages of dense bureaucratic gobbledegook, explaining how they must now be officially registered; how they might be inspected by a social worker at any time; and that anyone who 'obstructs' an 'authorised inspector' can be charged with a criminal offence. There then follow the most detailed instructions on how a playgroup should be run, to comply with the regulations. Exact specifications are laid down for the amount of floor space that must be available for each child – 3.7 square metres for each child up to two years of age; 2.8 metres for children of two to three years, and so forth – while of course 'it should be recognised that some children may be overwhelmed by too much space'.

The document requires that 'all rooms must be ventilated and kept at 18 degrees Celsius', and 'a thermometer should be mounted in a prominent place on the wall'. 'Children and adults should eat together in a way which promotes social and emotional development.' 'Children suffering from infectious diseases must be excluded from the centre in accordance with the exclusion periods specified by the Registration Officer' – except, the guidelines hasten to emphasize, any children who are 'HIV positive, who represent no threat to others (sic) health if high standards of hygiene are maintained at all times'. But what perhaps ring most oddly in the remote island community of Gaelic-speaking Presbyterians are the passages stipulating that: 'all materials should reflect accurately and positively the multi-cultural, multi-racial nature of British society. Stories and pictures should portray positive images of men and women playing a wide variety of positive roles'. Each child must be:

> valued as an individual without racial or gender stereotyp-
> ing . . . It is important that people working with young
> children are aware of this so that their practice enables the
> children to develop positive attitudes to differences of race,
> culture and language and differences of gender. The extent
> to which a centre is aware of and implementing equal

opportunities policies will be considered in the assessment for registration and at the point of inspection.

The intoning of such politically correct mantras in such a setting may recall how, only two years previously, the social workers of another island council, on Orkney, had organized dawn raids to snatch crying children from their homes, forcibly keeping them isolated from their parents for many months, for what was eventually recognized to have been no good reason.

* * *

It was not only in England that MAFF's new meat hygiene regulations were proving a disaster for the meat industry. Just before the following story appeared in the Sunday Telegraph, *in August 1992, it was reported that twelve slaughterhouses had closed in Scotland in the space of not more than a few weeks – all due to the new regulations.*

Nor-West Meats of Inverness is a meat cutting plant supplying butchers, hotels and hospitals all over north-west Scotland. During 1992, they are informed by MAFF officials from Aberdeen that, to comply with the Fresh Meat (Hygiene and Inspection) Regulations, they will have to make so many structural changes to their modern, purpose-built premises that they will have to be rebuilt, at a cost of over £750,000. In addition, they will have to pay for the full-time presence of a ministry-approved vet to supervise their operations, including the monitoring of temperature levels, at a cost of £60 per hour, or some £125,000 a year. In August 1992, the owner, Mr Robert Shaw, reluctantly concludes that his firm cannot afford all these charges and will have to close down, making twenty people redundant. A large local slaughterhouse, which has already spent a huge sum on modifying its own premises to comply with the new regulations, then discovers that it will lose fifty per cent of its business. In the nick of time it buys out Mr Shaw, so that Nor-West Meats can continue in operation. But the requirements of the regulations will still have to be met, at a cost which will render the once-profitable cutting plant uneconomical for years to come.

*   *   *

Nothing made more of a mockery of the EEC's policy to 'conserve fish stocks' than the way the quota system forced fishermen to dump huge quantities of dead fish back into the sea, because the 'quota rules' would not allow them to be landed.

Out in the North Sea in November 1992, while the Peterhead trawler Sundari is battling through mountainous waves, crewmen are struggling across the deck to throw overboard 300 boxes of fully-grown haddock, each box weighing more than a hundredweight. The skipper, Willie Morgan, and his men are having to dump their entire catch, worth £8000. This is because the yearly British quota for haddock under the EEC's Common Fisheries Policy has already been caught, and the fishermen know that if they bring the fish back into port they can be fined up to £50,000. Yet the reason why they cannot avoid catching this species is that there are more haddock swimming off the north-east Scottish coast in the autumn of 1992 than for many years past. Although the trawlermen are trying to catch whiting, every time they put down their nets they come up full of the forbidden haddock. Dozens of other trawler skippers are so desperate at the absurdity of the impasse to which they have been reduced by Britain's rigorous enforcement of the quota policy – designed to 'conserve fish stocks' – that they have to spend weeks from October to the end of the year tied up in port, losing earnings estimated at £1.5 million. Meanwhile out at sea, other European boats are catching almost unlimited quantities of haddock, knowing that their own fisheries inspectors will not be bothered by these ridiculous quota rules.

Britain was not in fact the only country to enforce the EEC's quota rules strictly, in a way which made a mockery of 'conservation'. We later spoke to Scottish fishermen employed on a Dutch trawler in the summer of 1993 who described how, in a five-week trip off the coast of Ireland, they had caught thirty million fish of species permitted under quota rules – and thrown back even more other species, including mackerel and herring, that were 'over quota'. This meant that, just from one boat on one trip, more than thirty million perfectly good fish were left to rot on the ocean floor. In 1993, such 'discards' broke all records, amounting to tens of millions of tons, thanks to the conservation policy devised by officials in Brussels.

*   *   *

Another problem vexing the Peterhead trawlermen at this time – as it does fishermen all over Britain – is the increasingly onerous burden of the 'safety inspections' to which they must submit their boats, carried out by officials from the Department of Transport. In 1992, the latest fashion among these inspectors is to demand that the propeller shaft be removed for examination. Not only has there never been any safety problem with propeller shafts, once they are removed they are notoriously difficult to replace securely. When skipper John Buchan, in the autumn of 1992, is made to remove the tailshaft of his trawler Fairline, nothing is found wrong with it. But over the next few months he three times has to cut short fishing trips because it is working loose. Four times he has to have it refixed. The whole exercise including inspection fees of £2000 ends up costing him nearly £10,000.

*   *   *

Farmers in 1993 were deluged with bureaucratic absurdities from Brussels. We have already seen something of 'set aside' and the IACS nightmare. We have also seen 'plant passports'. But even these paled beside the latest scheme dreamed up by the EEC and imposed with their usual cackhanded lack of efficiency by officials of MAFF – passports for animals.

In April 1993, at a cattle auction in Kildean, north of Sterling, David Dick, a local farmer, sells a year-old bullock for £650 to Mr and Mrs Gilman who farms down in Kent. As the sale takes place, several people at different stages have to read a plastic tag in the beast's ear, carrying the number SO102665B, and check against a piece of paper issued by the Scottish Office Agriculture and Fisheries Department (SOAFD) known as a Cattle Control Document (CCD), which is the animal's new 'cattle passport' (numbered 12/9040037591004922).

As from 1 April 1993, every one of the 1.8 million male cattle in the UK has had to have such a 'passport' under a new scheme imposed by the EEC. The claimed purpose of the scheme is to introduce a new system of paying subsidies on beef cattle, whereby payments are now made in two instalments, one when the animal is ten months old, the second when it is twenty-three months. But even though the scheme originated in Brussels, UK agriculture officials have managed to implement it in a uniquely cumbersome fashion, which for several weeks throws cattle sales in Britain into chaos.

Although farmers are threatened with loss of part or all of their subsidies if they make mistakes, in England and Wales thousands of farmers receive their forms weeks late – despite

MAFF's recruitment of 227 new officials to administer the scheme, at a cost of £5.3 million. Auctioneers predict that the system will be all but unworkable at large sales involving thousands of bullocks, each of which will have to have ear tags (of three different colours) read and checked several times against individual 'passports' (with their eighteen digit numbers) while the animals are pouring through the 'races' on their way from vendor to purchaser.

When it comes to claiming the subsidies, farmers stare in bewilderment at the formula set out in the glossy MAFF booklet on the 'Beef Special Premium': to qualify for payment, the farmer has to define his 'forage area' (five sorts of land excluded but remember not to exclude arable land on which 'arable aid' has not been claimed), and multiply that by the stocking density limit (3.5 livestock units, or LUs, per hectare in 1993, reducing by half an LU a year). Then the farmer must remember to subtract his number of dairy cows according to the following formula:

> Dairy cows calculated to be necessary to produce any milk quota you hold on 1 April of the year in which you claim Beef Special Premium of Suckler Cow Premium count against your total Livestock Units. The number of dairy cows is calculated using an average milk yield for the UK which is 5200kg (5050 litres) per cow for 1993. For example if you hold 60,000kg of quota on 1 April 1993 this will equal 11.54 dairy cows. One dairy cow is equivalent to one LU, so that is 11.54 LUs. You will have to subtract these 11.54 LUs from the total LUs available to you for the year as a whole . . . [etc, etc.]

No sooner have farmers been plunged into this latest instalment of insanity from the officials of MAFF and the EEC (coinciding with the even greater chaos of the new IACS

forms), than they have to prepare for another new requirement, under EEC Directive 92/102, on the 'identification and
registration of animals', which requires not just bullocks but
all cattle to have numbered ear tags. By the end of 1993, it
is proposed that every one of Britain's 11,788,000 cattle will
have to carry its own numbered tag – different from the ones
already issued to the beef cattle – and this time not just in
one ear but both, in case one of the tags is lost or damaged.

*   *   *

*Yet another time and money-wasting absurdity from the
Environmental Protection Act – as usual achieving no
environmental 'gain' whatsoever.*

Near Alnwick, Bob Harrison is forestry manager for the Duke
of Northumberland. On the estate they have a small sawmill,
cutting less than 5000 cubic metres of wood a year, and an
adjoining small workshop to treat the wood with preserv-
ative. Under Schedule 1, Section 6.7, Part B of the Environmental Protection (Prescribed Processes and Substances)
Regulations 1991, made under the Environmental Protection
Act 1990, as from October 1992, sawmills cutting more than
10,000 cubic metres of wood a year must be authorized by
the local council and become subject to detailed controls.
Because Mr Harrison's sawmill is well below the legal
threshold, he does not consider for a moment that he is
covered by the new regulations. But officials of the Alnwick
Council environmental health department rule that the sawmill and the treatment plant must together be regarded as
making up a 'process' and must therefore be 'authorised'.
This not only costs the initial 'authorisation fee' of £800,
plus a yearly 'subsistence fee' of £550. It also means that
the sawmill comes under the detailed control of the officials,
beginning with a requirement to pay £3750 a year to have

the sawdust 'analysed'. Each doorway to the plant has to have monitoring equipment installed to catch the sawdust for analysis. The official in charge orders Mr Harrison to keep the doors to the sawmill closed 'at all times' – until it is pointed out that they have to be opened to allow the wood in and out. Furthermore, every time sawdust is removed from the plant, under a section of the Environmental Protection Act, it becomes 'controlled waste'. 'Waste Transfer Notes' must be filled in, giving extensive details of each movement, and the sawdust – or 'particulate matter' as the officials call it – must be kept in sealed containers until it is off the premises; at which point the farmer who has bought it is free to do anything he likes with it, such as spread it on his fields. What Mr Harrison wants to know is – if sawdust from a nearby farm happens to blow back into the yard, and then blows out again into the fields, can the Duke of Northumberland be fined £20,000 under the EPA for allowing 'controlled waste' to pollute the environment?

*   *   *

At last we come to the end of the great 'wood is unhygienic' saga, with a surprising twist in the tail.

One of the most popular tourist attractions in Co. Durham is the open air museum at Beamish, showing life in a Victorian mining village. A particular highlight for the hundreds of thousands of visitors a year has long been a visit to the cottages next to the mine, where a lady dressed as a Victorian miner's wife cooks pies and cakes on a range in the kitchen. These look and smell so appetizing that in the summer of 1992 many visitors cannot help asking what happens to the food when it has been cooked. 'In the old days', they are told, 'we used to let every visitor have a taste. The children loved it in particular. But now we have to feed it to the animals on the farm.' When asked why, she explains that the pastry board and other implements in the kitchen are made of wood, and EHOs from Chester-le-Street Council have said this is not legal under the food hygiene regulations.

All over Britain in 1992, bakers, butchers, fishmongers, cooks and other 'food handlers' are being told that the use of wood is unhygienic and 'against regulations' – to be specific, Regulation 7 of the Food Hygiene (General) Regulations 1970. Millions of wooden spoons, chopping boards, rolling pins, shelves, brooms and other kitchen utensils have to be thrown away, while hundreds of millions of pounds have to be spent on the much more expensive plastic and metal alternatives favoured by the EHOs. All this obsession with the supposedly unhygienic nature of wood dates back to a study carried out in 1971 by Dr Richard Gilbert, who in 1992 is the head of the Public Health Laboratory Service food hygiene laboratory. He claims that plastic is easier to clean and preferable in every way, although this is often disputed by other experts, to no avail. But early in 1993, a new study is published in America by two scientists at the University of Wisconsin which seems to confirm that it is in fact wood which is much more hygienic, because it naturally has bactericidal properties, while plastic soon scores and builds up a coating of slime.

In June 1993, after the EHOs had forced hundreds of thousands of businesses in Britain to make a switch from wood to plastic, new advice was sent out to EHOs from LACOTS stating that the use of wood for chopping blocks and other implements was not an offence against Regulation 7 of the Food Hygiene (General) Regulations after all. It seemed that an end might at last be in sight for this remarkable bit of make-believe by the amateur 'hygienists'. But alas, British officials had long since infected their colleagues in Brussels

with the same disease, which meant that wood was now pro-
hibited in a whole string of EEC 'hygiene' directives – meat,
fish, poultry, game. The result was that, even though the UK
had at last come to its senses, many British businesses would
still be strapped into the 'no wood' straitjacket for years to
come.

* * *

At Billingham a medium-sized factory making potato crisps
for United Biscuits was in 1990 having to pay nearly
£300,000 a year to Northumbrian Water for the right to
discharge water from its production process into the sewerage
system. This was because the water contained small amounts
of chemical such as acetic acid (vinegar) which Northumbrian
water would have to remove in its purification process.
Alarmed by the size of this bill – United Biscuits like thousands of other companies has seen a sharp rise in its discharge
bill since the privatisation of the water industry – the firm
has spent £2.5 million on a sophisticated water treatment
plant to cut its emissions to a minimum. But in 1992 the sum
charged by the officials of Northumbrian Water rises to nearly
£600,000. The same thing is happening all over the country.
Although the water companies are careful to disguise the size
of their income from industrial discharges in their published
accounts, it is estimated that the cost to industry must now
be several billion pounds a year.

* * *

No industry in Britain faced a greater threat from the
Environmental Protection Act than the chemical industry.
Every one of Britain's thousands of chemical plants would
eventually require 'authorisation' to operate, from a body
of officials set up in 1989 with the imposing title of Her
Majesty's Inspectorate of Pollution. Negotiating these

authorizations would be a huge operation, lasting many years, and costing the industry billions of pounds. But HMIP began its work by requiring all new plants to be authorized immediately, before they could begin operating. The first of these to receive publicity, in the Sunday Telegraph, *was specially designed to be so 'environmentally friendly' that it only emitted a minute dose of 'pollutants' a year (as opposed to the 30,000 tonnes emitted annually by the plants on Teeside owned by ICI alone). This did not deter HMIP officials from treating it as if it was about to turn the whole of Middlesborough into a new Bhopal.*

On Teeside in January 1993, a new, £5 million chemical plant owned by Chemoxy International is standing idle whilst the company is having to turn away orders worth £60,000 a week. The plant is at a standstill because it is tied up in red tape by officials of HMIP. Using their powers under the EPA, they are enforcing a new regulatory system designed to limit pollution of the atmosphere by a range of chemicals known as VOCs, or Volatile Organic Compounds. Over the previous year, it has cost Chemoxy £120,000 in time, paperwork and fees just to get authorization from HMIP officials to operate the new plant at all. But the problem is made much worse by the particular nature of Chemoxy's work. As a contract company, it undertakes short-run chemical processing for some of the biggest chemical firms in the world, such as Bayer, Exxon and ICI. Every few days, therefore, it may need to change its process specifications. Each change requires fresh authorization from HMIP, which may take up to three weeks. Although the purpose of this bureaucracy is to regulate VOC pollution, the irony is that much of Chemoxy's work is recycling solvents, such as those used to de-ice windscreens, to make them less polluting. Furthermore, the plant is designed to be so 'environmentally friendly' that, when it is running

to full capacity, it will emit only some 8 kilograms of VOCs, such as acetic acid (vinegar), a year. This is much less than the quantity of VOCs emitted each year from the exhaust of the HMIP inspector's car on his visits to Chemoxy's factory. As the chemical industry — Britain's second biggest export earner — faces up to the implications of the grotesquely cumbersome new regulatory regime being imposed by HMIP, the Chemical Industries Association warns that Britain's 'ability to compete in the international market is already being significantly affected'. And, so far, the regulations only apply to new plants. When thousands of established plants are brought into the HMIP net over the next few years, it is feared that the industry may have to move large parts of its operation abroad to countries where no environmental rules apply.

*   *   *

In Northallerton, officials of the North Yorkshire Health Authority and the Hambleton District Council have, in July 1993, launched an important new health initiative. Ms Hazel Townsend, Senior Health Promotion Officer (HIV and Sexual Health) sends out a letter announcing that, as part of the local fight against 'the spread of sexually transmitted disease, including Human Immunodeficiency Virus (HIV)', she and Mr Kevin Hardisty, an EHO with Hambleton Council, are 'conducting a survey to establish the availability of condoms in the area'. 'To help us in our work', she writes, 'we would be very grateful if you can take a few minutes to fill and return the attached questionnaire'. When an incredulous local citizen calls to enquire whether this letter is a hoax, he is informed that 'the department' is 'most upset' at any suggestion that it might be being 'frivolous'.

*   *   *

Another example of how 'safety' measures demanded by the officials have made the world more dangerous.

At Wetherby races on Easter Monday 1993, jockey Neale Doughty is lucky to escape serious injury when his horse Algari bolts in the unsaddling enclosure, throwing him heavily against a stanchion. The reason for the horse's panic is that a spectator has brushed against a 'safety rope' installed across the enclosure on the instructions of an official of the Health and Safety Executive. Mr Doughty suffers severe bruising to his spine and Wetherby has suffered its first-ever off-course accident – as a result of 'safety measures' required by the officials. The course manager, Mr Christopher Tetley, orders that before the next day's racing, the rope should be removed.

*   *   *

In a comprehensive school in Bradford in April 1993, the head teacher issues his staff with a special notice to underline the ever-increasing problems caused by unruly and violent pupils. As teachers' powers to discipline pupils have gradually been eroded, the only sanction left is to 'exclude' pupils from the school by sending them home. During a recent ten-day period, the notice reports, thirteen pupils have been 'excluded', for offences ranging from use of 'obscene language' and 'threatening behaviour' to 'criminal damage' and 'possession of an offensive weapon' (the current fashion is to conceal a razor blade in an eraser). Being 'excluded' may not be such a burden to the teenagers concerned. It merely means that they can stay away to cause trouble on the streets. At least, however, it gives some respite to the teachers, who can get on with trying to teach, and to the pupils who want to pass exams. But now, it is reported, the officials of the Department for Education have come up with the brilliant idea of a new punishment. Not for the disorderly pupils but for the schools themselves. Those schools which go in for 'exclusion', the officials are suggesting, should be 'fined' to stop them using their only remaining power to keep any sort of order.

*   *   *

One of the most striking features of the 'enforcement blitz' of 1992 and 1993 was the sheer unpleasantness and arrogance shown by so many enforcement officials, given an inflated idea of their own importance by the new regulatory ethos of the time. Many of them were young, in their twenties, and a conspicuous proportion were female, only too quick to assert what the Jungian psychologists call their 'negative animus'. Although they had paper qualifications, they had little or no practical experience, and frequently showed a lamentable ignorance of the businesses and processes they were dealing with. Indeed, it almost became a rule of thumb that the more ignorant they were, the more they were likely to throw their weight around. We have already seen many instances of this (as in examples from South and North Pembrokeshire and Bolton). Here is another.

In Leeds, one day in 1992, a managing director of a small engineering works – a former naval officer who has been in charge of machinery and technical operations all his life – is up on a platform fixing a minor electrical fault in one of his machines. A young woman enters the factory and peremptorily orders him down to explain what he is doing. She is an official of the Health and Safety Executive. When he tells her, she asks him what his qualifications are. Having carried out similar repairs in his factory for twenty years, he is puzzled as to what she means. 'Have you got City and Guilds?' she asks. After racking his brains, he has to confess that he hasn't got any paper qualifications of the kind she

means. 'If I ever find you doing electrical work again', she says, 'I shall prosecute you', and storms out.

*　　*　　*

No one will ever know just how many 'food handling oper-ations' came to an end in the 'hygiene blitz' of 1992 – not just bakeries, fishmongers and butchers, but office kitchens, home-based cookery businesses, meals-on-wheels services, village halls, farm shops. The list was endless. What made this particularly horrifying was that in probably the majority of cases, the EHOs' demands had come way beyond the actual requirements of the law – as in these examples.

The people of Tadcaster in early 1992 are saddened by the disappearance from their market of the popular cheese stall, which for years has provided them with a wide range of top quality cheeses. Another disappearance at the same time is the van which has toured surrounding villages selling fish landed on the Yorkshire coast that morning, within hours of being caught. It emerges that both businesses have been forced to stop trading because EHOs from Selby District Council have told them that, under 'new hygiene regulations', the cheese must be refrigerated, and the fish man must now buy an expensive refrigerated van. In fact, there is nothing in the latest amendments to the food hygiene regulations which requires the refrigeration of either the cheeses or the fish. But such is the 'climate of fear and confusion' now created by the EHOs 'hygiene blitz' all over Britain that no one has been in a position to make this clear before the people of Tadcaster lost two of their most valued suppliers.

*　　*　　*

It was not only the meat trade that was savagely hit by the implementation of EEC 'hygiene' directives. A huge swathe

*of destruction was also cut through Britain's fish processing
industry.*

On Albert Dock, Hull, Selby & Mayes is one of the dozens
of firms of wholesale fish merchants which, for generations,
helped to make Hull one of the leading fishing ports of
Europe. Its premises are leased from Associated British Ports
and, in September 1992, they are inspected by Mr Kitching,
a Hull City EHO, to see whether they comply with the
requirements of the Food Safety (Fishery Products) Regulations 1992, implementing EEC Directive 91/493 which lays
down 'health conditions for the protection and placing on
the market of fish products'. The firm then receives a letter
stating that, unless it complies with thirty-one demands from
the EHOs, it will not be permitted to trade after 31 December
1992. Most of the demands are similar to those being made
by EHOs in respect of every kind of food business, all over
the country; walls, floors and ceilings must be 'smooth, easy
to clean, durable and impervious'; premises must be 'proofed'
against the entry of birds and insects with 'plastic strip cur-
tains' over all doors and windows; wood is 'unacceptable' for
any purpose; 'wooden filleting boards and wooden-handled
knives are prohibited'; and wooden benches must be replaced
by stainless steel. Many of these demands go further than the
strict requirements of the regulations so, on 3 October, Selby
& Mayes appeal. Six weeks later they have still had no reply
from the council. But the firm has been contacted by its land-
lords, Associated British Ports, who inform it that they are
not prepared to spend the money on 'bringing the premises
up to the standard required by the EEC fish hygiene directive'.
Selby & Mayes, like seven similar businesses in adjoining premises, therefore have no choice but to close down.
When local MP, Stuart Randall, is asked to take up their
case, he replies that there is nothing he can do because it is 'a

commercial matter'. All over Britain, hundreds of other fish merchants are going out of business for similar reasons.

*   *   *

Another example of the officials' craze for sending people on expensive and pointless courses – from which the only people to gain are the officials.

Near Barnsley, Richard Warttig has for twenty years run a turkey slaughterhouse. In 1992 he is informed by MAFF that, as from 1 January 1993, he will be required to hold a slaughterman's licence to stay in business. To obtain this, he will have to be instructed by a vet as to how the birds should be killed. This will cost him £200. To help defray the cost, Mr Warttig is permitted to round up several of his fellow turkey men, all of them experienced, and together they attend the lecture by a ministry-appointed vet. It turns out that this vet himself has only been on a two-week course and has infinitely less experience of slaughtering turkeys than any of his 'students'.

*   *   *

In Sheffield, George Gleadhill, John Johnson and John Bloodworth are butchers who each run small meat-cutting premises. In February 1993, they begin receiving daily visits from Mr Stewart, an official of the Sheffield City Council's Health and Consumer Services Department. Every morning, Mr Stewart carries out an 'inspection', leaving the owners with a list of 'requirements' which they have to sign. Frequently misspelled, these contain such items as 'Beems in chiller needs repainted', and 'no signiture when asked to sign'. When after several months the butchers raise this illiterate reign of terror with their local MP, Sheffield's Director of Health and Consumer Services, Mr Purcheon, assures him that MAFF guidelines require some businesses to be 'inspected daily'. In fact, the relevant ministry guidelines, FSH 4/92, specifically state that inspections of such premises need only be 'on a weekly or monthly rather than a daily basis'. Even more curious is that, in addition to the three butchers having to pay for Mr Stewart's time on their premises at £11.66 an hour, they also have to pay for his time driving to and from their premises. Although he visits them on the same round trip (two of the premises are adjoining), they note that each of them is charged for Mr Stewart's driving time and petrol. But the council officials make an important slip. The two businesses furthest from the town hall are each charged for '40 miles a month', whilst the nearest one is charged for '69 miles' as if a separate trip had been made.

*   *   *

All over Britain, motorists in 1993 were surprised by an unprecedented spate of road closures, often causing hold-ups or requiring diversions which added on half an hour or more to their journey. The explanation for this came to light with a particularly extreme example not long after the start of the year.

The 200 villagers of Conisholme on the Lincolnshire coast are startled to be told in January 1993 that, when resurfacing work is carried out to the A3101 which runs through their village, it will now be necessary 'under new safety regulations' to close the road completely for two weeks. Following the 'alternative route' suggested by the County Council, to drive from one end of the village to the other will now involve a forty mile journey. The local bus, which normally takes less than one minute to travel through Conisholme, will take an hour to make the same journey, via Louth and North Thoresby.

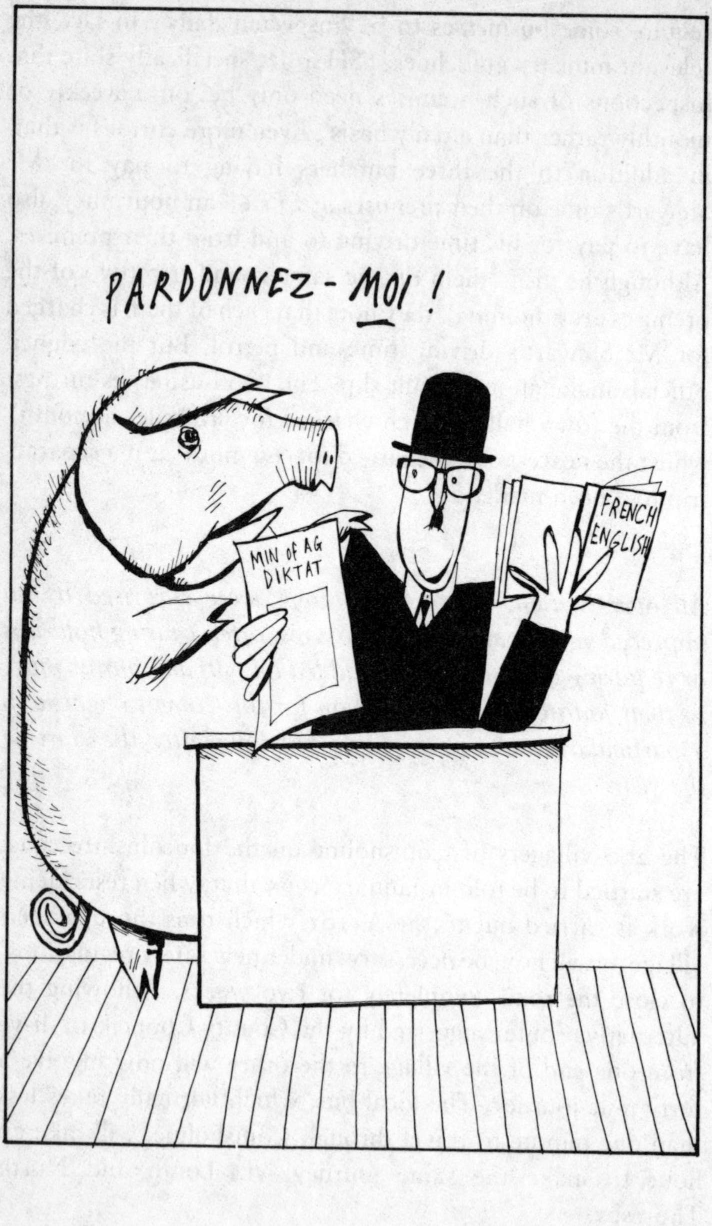
PARDONNEZ-MOI!
MIN OF AG
DIKTAT
FRENCH
ENGLISH

The reason for the horrendous inconvenience caused to the villagers is the coming into effect on 1 January 1993 of a new code of practice under the Health and Safety at Work Act 1974, laid down by the Department of Transport in Chapter eight of its 'Traffic Signs Manual', 'Safety Measures and Signs for Road Works and Temporary Situations'. This rules that there must now be a distance of 1.2 metres between the edge of any road works and the inner side of cones separating the workers from the traffic. Most of Britain's roads are not wide enough for this to allow even single-lane traffic. But as hundreds of thousands of motorists find themselves in 1993 delayed on their journeys, or sent miles off their normal routes into a maze of diversions, very few have any idea of the reason why.

*　　*　　*

Few 'Euro-absurdities' had a better claim to pass into folklore than the strange case of the mistranslation of just one word in a Brussels directive which cost an industry hundreds of thousands of pounds.

In Marcham Le Fen in January 1993, Eric Phipps, one of the county's best-known butchers, is launching a campaign to 'Save the Lincolnshire Chine', a traditional dish made from the stuffed forequarters of a whole pig. This famous local delicacy is threatened by a new diktat from MAFF, in its Fresh Meat (Hygiene and Inspection) Regulations 1992, which it claims are implementing the EEC's meat hygiene directive 91/497. The regulations lay down that all pigs must now be split down the middle for inspection before they can be sold. This has caused consternation not only in Lincolnshire but all over the country. Pig slaughterhouses have been paying out thousands of pounds for new mechanical saws, and one large company in the Midlands has even spent £50,000 on a new 'dressing line' to enable compliance with the regulations. But then it comes to light that the whole thing is a colossal misunderstanding. Five weeks earlier, on 27 November, Ray Mac Sharry, the EEC Agriculture Commissioner, has already written to a British MEP, explaining that the officials in Brussels had mistranslated one word in the original French version of the directive. The French wording had allowed for '*carcasses de porc*' to be inspected without being split. But in the English version, the word 'carcasses' has been given as 'heads'. Since this made no sense, when ministry officials in London came to draw up the UK regulations, instead of checking what was meant, they had simply included a requirement for carcasses to be split. Thus, the mistranslation of one word cost Britain's slaughterhouses hundreds of thousands of pounds. Even after the mistake had been detected, it takes MAFF until 21 January, nearly two months after the MacSharry letter, to acknowledge that a mistake has been made.

* * *

Another instance of the growing tendency of the courts to support overzealous officials.

In Stamford, Geoffrey and Patricia Tyers run a shop selling second-hand books and prints, with a newsagency and grocery shop at the front. In January 1992, while they are absent, a Mr Taylor enters the shop, describing himself as a 'team leader' for the local trading standards department. With the aid of a polaroid camera, he spends two hours examining the stock. In June, Mr and Mrs Tyers are summoned on twenty criminal charges under the Price Marking Order 1991, introduced by the DTI to comply with EEC Directives 88/314 and 88/315. It is alleged by the trading standards department that the twenty grocery items named were not price marked. The Tyers are very surprised. They spend much of their time in the bookshop at the back (where 10,000 books are each individually price marked). It is therefore in their interests that prices should be shown for all items in the grocery shop at the front, since this means that the assistants do not have to consult them. For most of the offences for which they have been charged, prices had been available nearby. For instance, sugar and orange squash had been priced on the shelf. Potato prices had been given on the vegetables price list. All crisps had been priced the same and, therefore, there was a single ticket stating this. Only three items had not had any prices nearby on the day Mr Taylor called, such as some milk which had only just been delivered (milk prices were on the fridge at the other end of the shop) and an old bottle of peppermint cordial, from which the price ticket had fallen off. When they arrive in court, the Tyers' solicitor says they will be offering a defence and the case is therefore adjourned for a full hearing. By the time this takes place, they have decided that they cannot afford more legal bills and will represent themselves. On arrival at court with a witness to support their claim that price marking was available for seventeen of twenty items, they find six people including a barrister representing the trading standards department. Outside the courtroom they are led to understand that if they plead guilty on some items, other charges will be dropped. They will have a chance to explain some of the mitigating circumstances (e.g. that price marking for most items was available nearby). The case, they are told, will be quickly over and, because this is new legislation, there will probably be only a nominal fine. In fact, they discover, although ten charges have now been dropped, they are both charged separately on each of the ten remaining charges, so they still face twenty charges. Because they have been persuaded to plead guilty, they are not allowed to introduce their witness to explain that price marking had been available for most items.

The magistrates fine them £30 on each of the twenty counts, a total of £600, plus £200 costs. On the same day, in a nearby court, a dangerous driver who has killed someone is fined £200.

* * *

What made the threat posed to hundreds of Britain's smaller abattoirs by the new meat 'hygiene' regulations particularly tragic was that these included many of the long-established craft slaughterhouses which produced the highest quality meat in the country. Here is a sad example.

In Farcet, Huntingdonshire, Tom Chamberlain runs a butchery business, owned by his family for 100 years. In 1992 he was champion sausage maker at the East of England Show and his business has never been more flourishing until, in December 1992, the busiest month of the year for butchers, he receives a letter from a MAFF official. This informs him that, under the new Fresh Meat (Hygiene and Inspection) Regulations 1992, he must make a number of structural changes to his premises. If he does not agree to this by 1 January 1993, he will not receive the new licence required by MAFF and will have to close down. His butcher's shop is twenty yards from his slaughterhouse across the yard, but he will no longer be allowed to carry meat across to it. He must build a refrigerated tunnel between the two buildings and a wall between his house and shop. In order to walk to work, he must now go out into the road and along the pavement. He must build a shower and a rest room for 'visiting lorry drivers', even though most of the animals arriving at his slaughterhouse come from farms within a five-mile radius. At weekends he is no longer permitted to drive his pride and joy, an old traction engine, past the slaughterhouse and shop. He must build a separate entrance for it. Quite apart from the irrelevance of all these demands to 'hygiene', the cost of complying would be so great that over the Christmas holiday Mr Chamberlain sadly concludes that he will have to close down his business forever. As Agriculture Minister John Gummer might have put it, he had taken 'a commercial decision not to invest in the future of his business'.

*   *   *

This is an instance of the suffering caused by 'politically correct' social workers which for once attracted national publicity.

In Cromer, businessman Jim Lawrence and his Asian wife Roma have applied to adopt a child. Because they are themselves from different racial backgrounds, they are hoping for a child of mixed race. But first they have to satisfy social workers of Norfolk County Council's Adoption and Family Finding Unit that they are suitable to become adoptive parents. Under their official guidelines, the social workers have to establish the attitudes of prospective parents to 'ethnicity' in a 'multi-racial culture'. Does 'each partner' adopt an 'anti-racist approach to parenting and how will this be demonstrated?' Team leader Terry Dunning asks Mrs Lawrence, as an Asian, about the difficulties confronting 'black' people in a 'racist' society such as Britain's. When she replies that she has never personally experienced problems of this kind, it seems that this is not the answer the social workers are looking for. A few weeks later, in July 1993, the Lawrences receive a letter saying that they have not been found suitable to adopt a 'black' or mixed race child, one of the main reasons being that they have not been able to show an understanding of the problems such a child would face. Shortly afterwards it comes to light that Mr Dunning had, nine years earlier, appeared on a television programme describing how he had confessed to his wife that he had fallen in love with a man called Philip. He had left his wife and two children to live the life of a homosexual. Asked to comment, Mr Lawrence says, 'Mr Dunning's sexual preferences are his own affair. But it is a matter of concern that someone who breaks up his own family can judge others who want to start a family of their own'.

*   *   *

For some reason, the EHOs seemed particularly proud of having been the first people in 500 years to discover that this Norfolk church tower was 'unsafe'.

The fifteenth-century church at Ranworth has 100,000 visitors a year, drawn partly by its famous painted medieval screen and partly by the unique panoramic view of the Norfolk Broads which can be seen better from the top of its tower than anywhere else. One day in April 1993, the vicar, the Revd Philip McFadyen, has a telephone call from an EHO of Broadlands District Council. The official says that he is serving an Emergency Prohibition Notice on the church tower. This means that it is being closed to the public immediately because it is 'unsafe'. It will be a criminal offence to allow anyone to climb it. The problem apparently is that there are no 'protective rails' on the stairs and the ladders on the way up the tower, and there are no guard rails to prevent visitors falling off the top. Mr McFadyen is dumbstruck. The Ranworth tower has stood for 500 years and there has never been any kind of accident. But he cannot argue with a statutory closure notice, and over the next six weeks sufficient measures are taken, including the placing of unsightly scaffolding round the tower roof, to persuade the EHOs to lift their prohibition. In the long term what they want is fibreglass baffles in all the gaps around the roof, which will cost the 100 villagers of Ranworth several thousand pounds to install. When this episode is reported in the EHOs' weekly magazine, *Environmental Health News*, as a triumph for the officials' tireless pursuit of the cause of public safety, it is given the headline 'Norfolk EHOs On A Mission For The Godly'.

*   *   *

We began this book with the crowning absurdity of the EEC's 'set aside' policy. Only in the summer of 1993 did it become clear just what a catastrophe it had been in practice.

In Thetford in July 1993, staff at the headquarters of the British Trust for Ornithology are contemplating one of the most horrendous wildlife disasters for years. During the spring and early summer of 1993, tens of thousands of farmers all over Britain were forced to 'set aside' fifteen per cent of their ploughland, under new rules brought in by the EEC to reduce crop surpluses. Inevitably, huge numbers of ground-nesting birds, such as skylarks, lapwings, partridges, yellowhammers and corn buntings, were attracted by the newly grassed and weed-covered fields and nested there. But under the rules drawn up by MAFF officials, farmers were told that they would not receive their 'set aside' subsidies of up to £130 an acre unless they mowed the land before 1 July, which is before the end of the nesting season. The result had been entirely predictable. As the machines moved in, eggs, chicks and sitting birds were destroyed. Preliminary estimates by the BTO show that the loss of skylarks alone has probably been as high as 250,000. Like most of the other species, these have been in sharp decline in recent years and the current UK population is only two million pairs. The only purpose of this holocaust has been to cut the yield of EEC cereal crops by fifteen per cent. But at much the same time, COCERAL, the European cereal growers organization, estimates that thanks to increased productivity on land still in cultivation, and manipulation of their crop mixes by farmers keen to maximise subsidies, the 1993 harvest will still be around 165 million tonnes, as against the 1992 total of 166 million tonnes, a drop of less than one per cent. The skylarks died in vain.

*   *   *

In a court at Bury St Edmunds in February 1993, businessman Anthony Jackson faces charges of 'damaging a scheduled ancient monument', namely a brick-and-flint wall only sixty years old. Mr Jackson owns a house adjoining the ruins of the medieval Mettingham Castle near Bungay, and in 1991 he had knocked a few inches off the top of the wall in his garden to get a better view. A neighbour had called the police, and when PC Boggis arrived on the scene he asked Mr Jackson to stop. Even though the wall was modern, it was officially classified as part of the 'ancient monument'. Since Mr Jackson refused to stop, he has now been prosecuted. The judge, Mr Stephen Solley, tells Mr Jackson, 'Nobody had clearer warnings than you. Your arrogance is beyond belief'. Mr Jackson is found guilty and fined £3000.

*   *   *

As debate raged over MAFF's forced closure of the slaughterhouses, no point was made more consistently by the minister responsible, John Gummer, than that this was necessary to ensure that 'consumers' were only given meat of the highest quality. Because he knew little of the science of the meat trade, he assumed that this came from modern 'factory abattoirs' which complied with 'EEC standards', presumably because he had been told this by his officials. He did not realize that top-quality meat came from the small craft slaughterhouses where prime animals could be treated individually, so that they were not 'stressed', and that they were killed by expert craft butchers. The meat from the mass-throughput abattoirs, where animals were herded through in a stressed condition, was for reasons of body chemistry likely to be tougher, and to last for a shorter time. Just before his new regulations were due to come into force, Mr Gummer's knowledge was put to the test.

In a small butcher's shop near Ipswich, George Debman presides over the enactment of a strange little drama in December 1992. All over Britain, hundreds of slaughterhouses are threatened with closure unless they can show that they meet the standards MAFF claims to be required for abattoirs under the Fresh Meat (Hygiene and Inspection) Regulations 1992, implementing EEC meat hygiene directive 91/497. Most of the slaughterhouses which already comply with the supposed hygiene and quality standards are large 'factory' abattoirs, processing thousands of animals a week. Those doomed by MAFF's interpretation of the regulations are the small and medium-sized craft abattoirs which produce the highest quality meat in the country, for sale to local butchers. At risk of closure in Debman's supplier, Colin Byford, who owns a slaughterhouse near Clacton. Byford has been told by MAFF that, if he wishes to stay in business at his present level, he must rebuild his premises at a cost of £350,000. In the forefront of the ministry's ruthless drive to promote the supposed 'hygiene and quality' standards has been Agriculture Minister John Gummer, who lives near Ipswich. He has been invited by Mr Debman to discuss the matter. Mr Debman shows the minister six samples of meat: pork, beef and lamb. Three are supplied by a factory-type abattoir, conforming with 'EEC standards'. The others come from Mr Byford's slaughterhouse. Mr Gummer, who has not been told of the origin of the meats, is asked to choose which of the six samples are, in his opinion, of the higher quality. Without hesitation, he picks the meat from Byford's slaughterhouse. Only then is he told its origin, and informed that the meat is two weeks older than that from the EEC abattoir. Far from being disconcerted by this demonstration that he knows nothing about the technicalities of the meat trade, Mr Gummer continues to support his officials in their devastating crusade to close down slaughterhouses like Byford's.

*　　*　　*

In Stevenage, Hertfordshire, the Warren Spring Laboratory, financed by the DTI, has for some time been causing anxiety among officials of the Department of the Environment for the independent way it carries out rigorous scientific investigations into the implications of environmental policies. In 1992, for instance, it has been researching the effect on Britain's crematoria of the D.o.E's new Guidance Note 52, made under the Environmental Protection Act 1990, which is intended to implement EEC Directive 84/360 on 'the combatting of air pollution from industrial plants'. According to the guidance note, crematoria are supposed to emit only 'one billionth of a gram per cubic metre' of 'dioxins' (chemicals which are given off from any domestic bonfire). This requirement poses enormous problems for the country's 240 crematoria, since only three are supposedly 'up to EEC standard', and it will cost upwards of £100 million to bring the rest into line. But when the Warren Spring scientists test one of the cremators which supposedly already comply with the D.o.E's guidance, it finds that it is still emitting between twenty-five and forty-five billionths of a gram pcm – up to forty-five times the legal limit. Even when the £100 million has been spent, therefore, it seems that all Britain's crematoria will still be breaking the law and should, strictly speaking, be prosecuted or closed down. Furthermore, Brussels is now planning to impose even tighter standards, reducing allowable emissions of 0.1 nanograms pcm, or one ten-billionth of a gram – a level so minute that the technology does not yet exist to measure it. It is perhaps hardly surprising that, when the Warren Spring report arrives at the D.o.E, there is a distinct silence from the officials for many months. But at least they are gratified to learn, in May 1993, that their counterparts at the DTI now have plans to close the Warren Spring Laboratory in 1994. This means they will be spared the embarrassment of having to cope with any more such reports in the future.

* * *

As hundreds of businesses crashed in the recession years of the early 1990s, a fact which escaped much notice was how many were wound up on the initiative of HM Customs and Excise. The VAT officials were so quick to send in the receivers that only later did it sometimes emerge that their reasons for doing so had been completely imaginary – as in this sad case.

In Grays, Essex, Peter Rimmell has in six years built up a printing business from scratch with a turnover in 1993 of £160,000. His customers include two local authorities and his local Labour Party. In May 1993, having fallen behind on his VAT payments for the first quarter of the year, Mr Rimmell is assessed by VAT officials as owing them £1700. They threaten that, unless he pays up by July, they will make him bankrupt. A week or two later, Mr Rimmell is visited by a VAT inspector, Mr Harris, who looks at his books and works out that the true debt is only £408.52. Mr Rimmell offers to pay this sum but is told that, because he is liable for a surcharge for late payment, he should wait until the total sum due has been worked out. On 23 July, having heard no more from the VAT office, Mr Rimmell is just about to go off on holiday with his girlfriend and her elderly parents when he is informed that he has been declared bankrupt. He is astonished, not least because an individual cannot be bankrupted for a sum less than £750. But it turns out that Customs and Excise have petitioned for bankruptcy on the £1700 originally assessed, even though it had been subsequently established that he owed much less. Mr Rimmell immediately contacts the Receiver, but is told that he must sort out the problem with the VAT office. There he is told he must talk to the solicitor handling the case, who is away sick. He leaves for his holiday but returns after the weekend to contact the solicitor – who is still away sick. Mr Rimmell obtains a promise from the VAT office that someone will contact him as soon as possible, and he resumes his holiday, leaving instructions for his staff to call him as soon as there is a message from the VAT office. After four days, when he calls his shop, a strange voice answers. It is an agent for the Receiver, who tells him that all his staff have been sacked and he must not come near his shop. In a state of shock, he rushes back from holiday to find that his premises are in chaos. Stock and cash are missing. A day or two later, printing machines worth £100,000 are removed from the shop. His £160,000 a year business is in ruins – all for a debt of not much more than £400, which he was willing and able to pay two months earlier. Mr Rimmell then learns that there has been an 'epidemic' of business bankruptcies initiated by Customs and Excise for VAT debt and that, according to one professional consultant, these are currently accounting for more than half of company winding-up orders in the London High Court.

* * *

We end with two stories about social workers. In the first, Teresa Gorman asks a question which could have applied to dozens of other examples in the book. Indeed it was a general question which had relevance to a great deal of what was happening in Britain in 1992 and 1993 (the other unspoken half of her question might have been 'what sort of a country do we have when the police are so busy filling in silly forms that they don't have time to catch real criminals?').

In the village of Orsett, Essex, Heather Armstrong has been running a nursery school in the village for twenty years. She has three helpers who have been with her for twelve years or more. Fees for each child are £5 a day for four mornings a week. In 1992 they are visited by a social worker from Essex County Council who informs them that the school must now conform with the requirements of the Children Act 1989. The hall must be fitted out with 'mini-loos' for the children, at £150 a time, 'mini-wash basins', 'mini-hand dryers', and 'mini-pegs' for coats. There must be new heating, play facilities out of doors — a whole string of demands with which neither the school nor the hall can afford to comply. Desperate to keep her school going, Mrs Armstrong explores every possible alternative, but to no avail. The social workers inform her that if she continues to run the school she and her assistants will be breaking the law and will be prosecuted on criminal charges. As MP Teresa Gorman asks when she raises the case in the House of Commons in January 1993, 'What kind of country do we have when silly regulations turn decent people, doing sensible and useful jobs, into criminals?'

*   *   *

In some ways this final story is the most horrifying in the book. It perfectly encapsulates the upside-down world which the officials inhabited — although in this case, because it violates something so basic to human reality as the love of a father and son, it provokes a special sense of outrage.

At Benfleet on a warm August evening in 1992, neighbours are astonished to see a 6-year-old boy, Peter Smith, being dragged kicking and screaming from his house by three social workers, headed by Mark Willis. Since his mother left home when he was three, Peter has lived alone with his father. On Sundays they go to church, and a fellow churchgoer says that the boy has always shown 'normal love and affection for his father and vice versa. It has always been our pleasure to see the obvious bond of a father and son'. At school Peter is regarded as 'a bright, well balanced, well loved boy' – according to his headmistress he is 'above average in intelligence'. Now he is being forcibly abducted from his father by the social workers, not because there is the slightest allegation that he has been abused or mistreated but because the social workers have decided that Mr Smith has not been providing his son with 'enough emotional and intellectual stimulation'. Using their powers under the Children Act, the social workers place the boy in a foster home. It later emerges that Mark Willis, leader of the team which has been empowered to treat the boy in this fashion, has subsequently returned to college to continue a course in social work. He is not even yet a fully qualified social worker. It also appears that this is by no means the first time in Essex social workers have removed children from their parents for similar reasons. In another case, reported at length in the *Spectator* by Alasdair Palmer, two parents are described talking of how their world has fallen apart since their two sons were removed by the social workers, also for failing to give them 'emotional and intellectual stimulation'. One boy had been fostered out with another social worker. The other had reacted very badly to being removed from his parents, had become increasingly disturbed and unruly and had ended up being placed in an institution. In the case of Peter Smith, only after intensive lobbying by local MP Dr Bob Spink is the case eventually referred to a

judge. Six months after he has been kidnapped, by officials using the full powers of the state, Peter is returned to the father whom he has several times been told he would 'never see again'.

*   *   *

At this point our tour of Britain has come full circle. We began in Essex with Chesterton's story of the mother snatched away from her children, not because she had maltreated them but because local officials thought living in their dirty cottage might not be good for their health. We end back in Essex eighty years later with the boy being snatched away from his father, not because he had been maltreated but because local officials thought he was not receiving enough 'stimulation'.

Two things inspired Chesterton to one of his finest flights of outrage in The Mad Official. *The first was the total lack of connection between the supposed 'problem' and the 'remedy'. The second was that, when something took place so bizarrely at odds with humanity and common sense, the world could apparently carry on as if nothing had happened. A society truly going off its head, as Chesterton wrote, is one where such things can happen every day and no one takes any notice.*

Such was the case with Britain in 1992 and 1993, as we have seen in the 140 stories in this book (for each of these we would have had little difficulty in finding a dozen more). What they have in common is not just the power of the state being used officiously and arrogantly, but officials acting in a way that defies the reality of the causes they are serving – 'hygiene', 'safety', 'environmental protection', 'caring' and the rest. Yet, even though many such stories received fleeting attention from the press, what was significant was how the media seemed by and large quite unable to see the connection between individual instances, and how they were all symptoms of something much deeper and more general that was happening in our society. What we were seeing was a huge explosion of bureaucracy and bureaucratic modes of thought, extending its influence into almost every aspect of life – a monster out of control, not just because it was inflicting immense damage on businesses and people's lives, but because so much of what it was doing was totally irrelevant to any real problems. Nothing brought this home more clearly, as we shall see in the next chapter, than when a real problem emerged, affecting hundreds of thousands of people and crying out for the most urgent action by the government. Faced with a genuine disaster involving health and safety, official-dom could not run fast enough in the opposite direction.

PART 3

THE MONSTER EXPOSED

As our investigation proceeded, we began to uncover one disaster unfolding in the Britain of 1993 that was of quite a different order from anything else we had been looking at.

We were first introduced to it in the unlikely setting of the House of Lords in early May 1993, by an interview with the Countess of Mar, the thirty-first holder of the ancient Scottish earldom of Mar, the oldest title in the UK. The Countess described how, on her farm in Worcestershire, she kept sheep. Since the mid-1980s, like all Britain's other 95,000 sheep farmers, she had been compelled by MAFF to dip her animals twice a year against two particularly nasty parasitic diseases, scab and blow-fly. Like the vast majority of farmers, the chemical she used, approved by MAFF's Veterinary Medicine Directorate, were organo-phosphorus compounds, known as OPs.

Although the instructions said these should be handled with care, it is very difficult when sheep are being manhandled through a dip-tank not to breathe in the vapour, or get the odd splash – or even, as Margaret Mar did in 1989, to have some spill into a boot. A week later she began to suffer head-aches, dreadful tiredness, acute muscular pains and depression, which got worse. She had problems with speech and vision, memory lapses, her brain going 'woolly'. A succession of doctors told her it was just 'menopause', 'shingles', 'ME syndrome', even that it was 'all in the mind' and that she should see a psychiatrist.

Only two years later, in 1991, did she learn, almost by chance, that her symptoms were the classic syndrome of chronic poisoning by organo-phosphorus chemicals – and that these had originally been developed in Nazi Germany as a nerve agent for chemical warfare. OPs work by eroding the nervous and immune systems – hence their efficiency as pesticides. The Countess had suffered damage to her health which was 'permanent, irreversible and untreatable'.

The Countess then discovered that she was far from being alone – not least from a remarkable woman, Liz Sigmund, who had been running a campaign from her home in Cornwall to promote awareness of the dangers of OPs. Thousands of other farmers had been afflicted by the same problem in recent years. Many had suffered even worse than herself, becoming paralysed, being forced to take to a wheelchair or give up farming, having to be admitted to mental hospitals or being hit by depressions so severe that this could be a factor in the epidemic of suicides which had put farmers second only to vets as the most suicide-prone group in the community. A random sample of sheep farmers investigated by the National Farmers' Union in the south-west in 1991 showed that thirty-five per cent reported symptoms of poisoning, and that its effects could be cumulative.

Yet the oddest thing about this disaster was the attitude of officialdom. As long ago as 1951, an official report written for the Ministry of Agriculture by Solly Zuckerman had warned of the extreme dangers of OPs. Twenty years later, however, MAFF had been making their use virtually compulsory for sheep farmers, with almost none of the safety precautions by this time obligatory for products nothing like so dangerous. They had been approved by MAFF's Veterinary

Medicines Directorate, advised by a supposedly independent Veterinary Products Committee, eleven of the seventeen members of which in 1992 had professional links with pharmaceutical companies which made OPs. Through its Veterinary Medicines Directorate, MAFF had maintained that it was primarily the responsibility of the chemical manufacturers to indicate to farmers what precautions they should take. They had scarcely gone out of their way to emphasize the dangers, and although the VMD had set up a system whereby farmers could report 'suspected adverse reactions' from chemicals used on farms, this presented them with such a bureaucratic maze that few of the farmers affected could overcome the hurdles placed in their way (even so, in 1992, the VMD admitted that the number of reports had nearly quadrupled in a year, from sixty-three to 227, and that 154 of these had related to OPs).

Another body involved in this drama was the Health and Safety Executive, responsible for the COSHH regulations and safety in the workplace in general, and normally only too eager to exercise its regulatory powers. Indeed in 1981, the HSE had published a booklet MS17 in its medical series, which provided the fullest clinical guide to the dangers and diagnosis of OP poisoning available in Britain. Yet twelve years later the HSE seemed curiously embarrassed by this document, and when it came to taking any action to regulate the use of OPs, or to investigate incidents where OP poisoning was suspected to have occurred, its officials seemed to have become afflicted with a mysterious paralysis. A similar paralysis seemed to have seized the medical profession. All over the country GPs were remarkably reluctant to accept that sheep farmers could be suffering from the effects of these chemicals, even when they were desperately ill. Like the Countess of Mar, they were told that they must be suffering from anything but the well-attested symptoms of OP poisoning; that their problems must have arisen from some unidentified 'virus'; that it was a 'psychiatric matter'; even that they were alcoholics. When in the summer of 1993, the Chief Medical Officer at the Department of Health belatedly sent a letter to GPs on sheep-dip poisoning, he merely included a leaflet drawn up by two bodies funded by the pharmaceutical companies on how to carry out dipping 'safely'. This contained neither clinical guidance on diagnosis nor details on treatment. Where, from all these official bodies, one might in normal circumstances have expected a concerted programme of research, the most severe controls, a full publicity campaign to warn of the dangers, the sheep farmers were being left to struggle on alone with the consequences of an appalling tragedy, surrounded by what seemed to amount on all sides to a conspiracy of official silence.

Furthermore, we soon discovered that the consequences of this tragedy were not confined to the farmers themselves. Liz Sigmund put us on to Brian Anderson, living near Blairgowrie in Perthshire. Until 1989, when he was in his early forties, he had been extremely fit and active, running a successful Christian community in the Perthshire hills, coaching the local rugby team and helping to support the community financially by selling flowers and vegetables from the garden he worked himself. Earlier he had been a driving instructor for the Metropolitan Police, and before that he had worked for the Botswana government in charge of policing the northern half of the Kalahari Desert. But in October 1989 he had fallen seriously ill after drinking water from a hillside well, and eventually discovered that this might have been contaminated by OP sheep-dip used by a neighbouring farmer. Certainly Mr Anderson suffered from all the symptoms associated with severe, chronic OP poisoning – extreme pain and weakness, severe depression and hallucinations, such as imagining that he was being repeatedly run down by an InterCity train. By

1993 he was so ill that he was virtually unable to work at all.

Yet, being an intelligent and very determined man, Mr Anderson had lodged a formal complaint with the European Commission in Brussels, that the British government had been allowing these dangerous chemicals to be disposed of in a way which was in breach of two EEC water quality directives. In May 1993, the Commission served notice that it was embarking on legal procedures which could end in the UK government being taken to the European Court of Justice. Privately, experts in Brussels said that they were 'amazed and horrified' that the British government had permitted the use of such dangerous 'neurotoxins' at all.

If OPs were getting into water supplies, how many other people might be affected? We discovered that in 1991 Tony Coddington, a senior scientist with the National Rivers Authority, had been so concerned by this question that he had carried out an extensive study. This showed that OPs were contaminating some water supplies to an extent well in excess of legal limits. His report had been sent to MAFF in November 1992, and was followed by a deafening silence. We also learned from the Confederation of Wool Textile Manufacturers in the summer of 1993 that OP residues in water supplies were beginning to pose an immense problem to Britain's carpet industry. The NRA had been finding that OP residues washed out of wool used in carpet factories were way above the limits permitted by new EEC legislation coming into force after 1 January 1994, and the carpet manufacturers could see no way in which they could comply with these limits; the problem went back to the impregnation of the wool by dipping, which was beyond their control.

The further our investigations continued, the wider we discovered the ramifications of this disaster to run. We received a letter from Professor Peter Behan, a neurologist at Glasgow

University, who for some years had been engaged in possibly the most extensive research project in the world into the mysterious ailment known as ME, which was now affecting more than 150,000 people in Britain. The symptoms of ME were remarkably similar to those of OP poisoning. And what had particularly struck Professor Behan and his team in the course of their researches was the number of ME victims they had studied who turned out to have been exposed through their occupation to organo-phosphorus chemicals.

Sheep-dipping is in fact only one of the countless ways in which the modern world has come to rely on OPs for their pesticidal properties. Back in the 1960s, when the world woke up to the environmental disaster which had been caused by the post-war generation of pesticides based on organo-chlorine compounds, such as DDT and dieldrin, hopes for a new chemical 'golden age' came to be pinned on organo-phosphorus compounds, the environmental effects of which were supposedly less damaging because they were less persistent in soil and water. So complete had the switch been that, by the 1990s, OP compounds formed an active agent in well over half the products listed in the World Pesticides Guide, used for a wide range of purposes all over the world. Although in the most developed countries, such as the USA, their potential danger to human beings was freely acknowledged and their use tightly regulated, this for some reason did not seem to be true to anything like the same extent in Britain.

Not only were we ourselves now coming across more and more apparent victims of OP poisoning who had nothing to do with sheep-dipping; people had become affected by drift from agricultural sprays; by insecticidal spraying of homes, hospitals or bakeries; by the use of OPs in gardens and greenhouses; even by their use in flea collars for pets. Even more alarming was to discover just how easily OPs could enter the food chain. We were given eyewitness accounts of vegetables and fruit being sent to supermarkets still seriously contaminated with OP sprays. We were given evidence of how milk and meat could be contaminated by a whole range of OP treatments used on cattle and sheep. A report by the British Medical Association in 1991 had referred to a study which established the remarkable extent to which the residues of OPs used to protect grain in storage remained in flour used for baking bread. And one thing which was inescapable was how similar the symptoms of organo-phosphorus poisoning were to those of the many mysterious ailments which have been so markedly on the increase in recent years; not only ME but certain types of cancer, asthma (which despite its often trivial nature, can also be fatal) and allergic sensitivities of every kind.

It seemed that what we were facing might be a public health disaster so immense that the tragedy of thalidomide would look tiny in comparison.

*   *   *

The contrast between the picture we have been looking at in the last few pages and that presented earlier in the book could scarcely be more glaring. On the one hand, in response to various scares and concerns of the late 1980s, an avalanche of legislation had created a regulatory apparatus unlike anything seen in our society before. Armies of officials had swarmed across the nation, inflicting untold financial damage, closing down successful business, turning peoples' lives into a nightmare, for no good reason whatsoever. The sound of sledgehammers being wielded to miss nuts was deafening. On the other hand, when a genuine catastrophe emerged, closely related to those same noble causes of health and safety, the environment and caring, the sledgehammer was nowhere to be seen. The only sound was that of the shuffling of official papers, as the bureaucrats and regulators tried to pretend the problem did not exist.

As we saw in the introduction, when this unprecedented onslaught of new regulation from Brussels, Whitehall and the town halls first began to arouse public alarm in the autumn of 1992, even the politicians soon became aware that something very odd was going on. Immediately the cry went up that what was wanted was 'deregulation'. This was chosen as the theme for the Conservative Party conference at Brighton in 1992. Over the next few months, seminars were held at 10 Downing Street, involving the entire Cabinet. A special 'Scrutiny Unit' was set up in the DTI to report how EEC directives were transposed into law. Seven 'task forces' of businessmen were launched to report on how different industries could benefit from 'deregulation'. We were told that there was no issue which the prime minister viewed with more concern.

But if there was always a curious air of unreality about this frenzy of deregulatory chatter, it was not least because the government so passionately proclaiming the virtues of deregulation was the same government which had called most of the damaging legislation into being in the first place. In the very year when John Major was calling at Brighton for the need to 'hack back' the jungle of red tape and 'bloody-minded petty bureaucracy', his own government was breaking all records for the number of new regulations pouring out of the machine. In 1992, the number of 'statutory instruments' passed on the nod through parliament soared to a historic high of 3359, 407 more than the previous record established in 1991, equivalent to ten new sets of regulations every day. And when the same politicians now talking high-mindedly of their desire to 'deregulate' were asked about any specific piece of regulation that was causing damage, it was strange how quickly their officials could provide them with eloquent reasons as to why this particular measure was amply justified – or there was nothing they could do about it because it had all been 'agreed in Brussels' and therefore their hands were tied. Again and again, businessmen attempting to discuss their problems with ministers reported that it was like talking to them 'through a glass wall'. They simply did not understand.

To those of us observing this process closely in 1993, it seemed that most politicians had quite lost any capacity for independent thought about what was going on. They had passed entirely into the hands of their officials. There was once a time when the British civil service and administrative machine, both at a national and local level, had rightly been the envy of the world. Vestiges of this survive – dedicated, intelligent and sensible civil servants and officials can still be found. But what the politicians could not in the 1990s appreciate was the extent to which the system had been corrupted. What their new legislation had called into being was a hugely expanded regulatory machine which in many respects had now gone completely off the rails. Faced with evidence that, in practice, it was simply no longer working and was causing incalculable havoc, they could only fall back on reiterating the theory behind it, as if such wishful thinking was the only reality they could grasp. Most serious of all, when they tried to respond to the mounting public pressure to curb the monster's excesses, whom did they consult as to how this might be done but the very people who had most to gain from the growth of the monster's power and self-importance, the officials themselves.

One particularly sinister phenomenon we identified in the course of our investigations was the SEFRA, the Self Financing Regulatory Agency. Under the influence of the government's wish to cut down the numbers of the civil service and public spending, there had for some years been a growing tendency to hive off parts of the civil service into independent agencies which, wherever possible, had to be self-financing. When these were armed with regulatory powers, a very dangerous mix emerged, to the consequences of which the politicians seemed largely oblivious. All across the regulatory spectrum we could see these bodies emerging – the National Rivers Authority, Her Majesty's Inspectorate of Pollution, the Waste Regulatory Authorities, the Planning Inspectorate, the Fishing Vessel Survey, the Data Protection Agency, the agencies set up under the Financial Services Act, the Medicines Control Agency, to name but a few. They had the power to 'authorise' anything from the discharging of water into a river, to the running of a chemical plant, from the manufacture of a drug to the running of an insurance company, from the keeping of electronic data to the right to take a fishing boat to sea. And what distinguished the SEFRA was not only its powers to impose regulations on business or other forms of activity, but that it should pay its own way by charging fees for compulsory licensing or registration. It could impose penalties for non-compliance, ranging from fines to closure, or the withdrawal of licences, which had the same effect. And it could often act as its own arbiter, in that there was no appeal in law against many of its decisions.

If all this seemed desirable to the government for one reason – in that it drastically cut the cost of regulatory activity to public funds – there was another reason why it was so appealing to the officials themselves. Quite apart from the sheer enjoyment of bureaucratic empire-building and the exercise of power, they could look forward to remarkable increases in their salaries. When, for instance, the Medicines Control Agency, responsible for authorising the manufacture of drugs, was still part of the D.o.H in 1991, its staff were on civil service salaries. It was run by a Mr Jones, on a 'Grade 3' salary of £49,000. In 1992, however, when the MCA had become an independent agency, its 'profits' from licensing and inspection fees doubled, from £9 million to £18 million. Mr Jones's wages rose to £78,000 – and the number of his staff on salaries between £40,000 and £50,000 rose from thirteen to thirty. A similar picture emerged from SEFRAs across the board – and of course this meant that the officials had a vested interest in increasing their own regulatory powers and the charges that went with them.

It was scarcely surprising, therefore, that the officials were so keen on SEFRAs, and continually pressing for new ones to be set up. One of their chief aims for the 1990s is the setting up of a huge environmental agency, rather on the model of the American Environmental Protection Agency, made up from a merger of the NRA, Her Majesty's Inspectorate of Pollution and the Waste Regulation Authorities, with some of the current pollution control role of EHOs thrown in. In MAFF, there seems to be a similar strategy to set up a UK equivalent to the Food and Drugs Administration, which would have responsibility for all matters relating to 'food safety'. This will begin by hiving off meat inspection in the UK to a 'National Meat Hygiene Service' with 1800 officials to regulate the meat and poultry industries, and imported foods. But in due course, if the officials get their way, this could extend its powers to many of the other responsibilities currently exercised by MAFF's Food Safety Directorate, also taking over some of the roles of the D.o.H and EHOs. If it can then extend its powers to charge for registration and inspection, as the National Meat Hygiene 'Service' is already planned to enjoy, another hugely powerful SEFRA will have been born.

In this context, it was particularly interesting to note how the officials cleverly hijacked even Mr Major's deregulation drive to further their long-term plans. When the 'Scrutiny Unit' of seven officials reported on the way in which the EEC meat hygiene directive had been implemented in the UK, its central recommendation was that the National Meat Hygiene Service should be set up straight away, even though the formation of the service was not part of the Scrutiny brief. So determined were MAFF officials to push on with their secret strategy that even the deregulation exercise could be used as a cover to plan a massive increase in the power and influence of the regulators. Deregulation equalled regulation. The Orwellian equation was complete.

Against such Machiavellian single-mindedness, what hope did the politicians have? It is true that, in the face of various campaigns to publicise the extent to which the monster was running out of control in 1993, there were signs here and there that the seemingly unstoppable momentum of the previous few years was being checked. Faced with a barrage of criticism, the monster drew in its horns in a number of directions. In February 1993, MAFF was forced to put an end to the fiasco of its compulsory testing of egg-laying flocks for salmonella, and the policy which in four years had involved the slaughter of more than three million chickens, driving more than 5000 producers out of business for no benefit whatever. A relentless battle to expose the disasters EHOs were inflicting on 500,000 food handling operations led to the government making a number of moves to curb their excesses, and to persuade them to be less aggressively confrontational. There were new guidelines to curb the absurdities inflicted by social workers on thousands of playgroups and care homes. There were brave declarations that we would not be pushed around by so many Euro-directives, and that we would try to insist on other Member States implementing and enforcing Euro-legislation more rigorously.

But what inevitably prompted the suspicion that these might be merely tactical withdrawals, an exercise in damage limitation, was that in none of these cases was there any official admission that a catastrophic blunder had been made. There was no sign that the real nature of the great regulatory disaster had been recognized; that in terms of realizing its declared aims, the whole regulatory operation might have been totally misguided, from top to bottom. And what of course brought home more than anything the surreal nature of the world this had been bringing about – Alice in Wonderland crossed with Kafka – was the genuine catastrophe being inflicted by organo-phosphorus chemicals. The health of possibly tens of thousands of people had been irreparably damaged – and the officials had not wanted to know. They had allowed it to happen. They had actively helped to bring it about. And their energies had been so happily diverted into the displacement activity of persecuting egg farmers, slaughtermen and hundreds of thousands of other businesses that, when the disaster finally began to emerge, their only instinct was to indulge in a colossal cover-up.

This more than anything brought home the thin, two-dimensional unreality of the great debate on deregulation, which was so often presented by politicians as though it was just a matter of hunting down a few hundred silly and usually obsolete bits of red tape, and then with a great flourish pronouncing that they might one day be abolished.

What the OP disaster so clearly demonstrated was that what Britain really needed was not so much deregulation but reregulation, a rethink of the whole system to ensure that regulation was switched away from all this costly and damaging displacement activity and redirected to where it was genuinely needed. Here, if anything, was a perfect example of where the most stringent regulation was called for, based on proper investigation, proper science and a proper sense of care and responsibility for the health and wellbeing of enormous numbers of people. But this, as we hope the book has shown, is not the monster's concern or its way of doing things. This is why we are forced to conclude that, despite attempts to argue to the contrary, the monster is still running out of control. It may have been bruised here and there by criticism. It may have made its placatory gestures by way of damage limitation. But essentially, it has not changed its nature one jot. It is still there, balefully, watching for the chance to resume that one great, overriding mission which justifies its existence and everything it does – simply to exercise its powers, and wherever possible to extend them. It can do this above all because the British people as a whole, the politicians and the media, have not yet really begun to wake up to just what a disaster is in the making. What is needed is a national awakening to the nature of the monster which has come into being, and just how, where and why our regulatory system has gone wrong. At the end of 1993, it seems that the awakening is still very far off.

ACKNOWLEDGEMENTS

If this book had a dedication it would be to all those thousands of readers of the Sunday and Daily Telegraphs whose letters have helped us more than anything else to build up a picture of the 'regulatory disaster' falling on Britain in 1992 and 1993. It has only been possible to use a small proportion of their stories in this book but we would particularly like to thank:

Nick Adames; Bert Adams; Stephen Alambritis (Federation of Small Businesses); Revd Brian Anderson; Mira Bar-Hillel; Mrs Gillian Baring; Revd Leslie Barnard; Bill Bates; Nigel Batts; Bob Baxter; Professor Peter Behan; John Brace; Roger Brown; Peter Buckley; Jane and Eric Burke; Tim Butcher; Robert Butterworth; Colin Byford.

Bryan Cassidy MEP; Viscount Coke; John Connor; Barry Cotter; John Curtiss; Mrs Margaret Daly MEP; Nick Dark; George Debman; Lord Deedes; Leon Downey; Roger Eddy; Liz Elliot; Will Ellsworth-Jones; John Evans; Andrew Fairweather; Mike Fisher; Christopher Gilbey; Christopher Gill MP; Dr Anthony Gilham; Teresa Gorman MP; Richard Green; Elizabeth Grice; Andy Griffiths; Paul Griffiths; Elizabeth Gundrey (*Staying Off The Beaten Track*).

Alan Halsall; Neil Hamilton MP; Bob Harrison; Tim Hart; Duff Hart-Davis; Malcolm Headley; Norman Henry; Susan Hinton; Mrs Beverley Houlford; Richard Ingrams; Dr Nick James (Chairman, Paddle Steamer Preservation Society); Jill and Antony Jay; Jean Jackson; Hon. Tessa Keswick; Lord Kilmaine; Libby King; Leo and Polly Kirk; Jenny Lacey; Mrs Margaret Leonard; Geoff Lewis.

Heather Macaulay; John Macleod; Mick and Joan Mahon; the Countess of Mar; Roger Martin; Errol Mason; Julian Miller; Austin Mitchell MP; Adam Nicolson; Mrs Mary North; Tim Oliver (Editor, *Fishing News*); Hugh Oliver-Bellasis; Robin Page; Michael Pearce; Willy Poole; Keith Pulman; Graham Rhodes; Ian Rodger; Dr Philip Rose.

Mrs Sally Scrope; Mary-Anne Sieghart; Elizabeth Sigmund; Mrs Vivienne Sinkins; Mrs Christine Smedley; Ian Smedley; Clem Shaw; Anthony Steen MP; Brian Stenhouse (President, British Beekeepers' Association); Brien Symes; Mrs Helen Thomas; Elwyn Thomas; Miss E. Tucker; Colman Twohig; Geoffrey and Patricia Tyers; Paul Vallely; Lord Vinson; Ernest Virgo; Roddi Vout; Mrs Jane Wakeham; Richard Warttig; Julian and April Westcott; Mrs Joanna Wheatley; Professor Verner Wheelock; Freda Williams; Mrs Joan Wood; Dr Robert Woodward; Charles Wyatt.

We are also indebted to the following publications: the *Sunday Telegraph*; the *Daily Telegraph*; *The Times*; the *Daily Mail*; the *Independent*; the *Daily Express*; the *Evening Standard*; the *Observer*; the *Spectator*; *Private Eye*; the *Grimsby Evening Telegraph*; the *Glasgow Herald*; the Basildon *Evening Echo*; *Fishing News*; *UKEPRA News*; *Farmers' Weekly*; and other provincial newspapers in which many of these stories were first reported.

INDEX